How You See Me

WRITTEN BY

JULENA C. G.

(JUJU)

Copyright © 2024 by Julena Coleman-Gillam

All rights reserved.

No part of this publication may be reproduced, distributed, or transmitted in any form or by any means, including photocopying, recording, or other electronic or mechanical methods, without the prior written permission of the publisher, except in the case of brief quotations embodied in critical reviews and certain other noncommercial uses permitted by copyright law.

This book is a work of fiction. Names, characters, places, and incidents are products of the author's imagination or are used fictitiously. Any resemblance to actual events, locales, or persons, living or dead, is entirely coincidental.

Table Of Content

Introductory 1

Chapter 1- I see you in me 4

Chapter 2 Faith got me through doors that fear couldn't 9

Chapter 3 How you see me 13

Chapter 4 You have to know the beginning to understand the end 20

Chapter 5 Change atmospheres 27

Chapter 6 The nightmare that still haunts me 36

Chapter 7 What do you do when you can't do anything? 44

Chapter 8 Questions I never received answers for 52

Chapter 9 The transition 58

Chapter 10 Sex, lies and drugs 67

Chapter 11 It was all a dream 72

Chapter 12 Money, Power, No Respect 78

Chapter 13 Be careful who you call a friend 83

Chapter 14 What's freedom? 89

Chapter 15 Ready or not 96

Chapter 16 Adulthood isn't as fun as I thought it'll be 102

Chapter 17 Lemons and lemonade 110

Chapter 18 Finding another way 115

Chapter 19 This is where it begins 122

Chapter 20 Jumping 129

Chapter 21 The importance of accountability 137

Introductory

Hi, my name is Julena, also known as "Juju or Ju" for those who do not know me already. Julena and Ju are completely different people, almost like sisters living in the same body. Now, I know what you're thinking; this girl is absolutely crazy. I'm not about to read a book about a crazy chick. I am not crazy. Well, I haven't been medically diagnosed as such, anyway. In my book, I may make you laugh, smile, cry, or help make you richer. My goal is to motivate and encourage you. I realized years ago that my purpose in life is to inspire and give light to individuals who may seem like they are living in the dark or struggle to see the gift of life.

Growing up, I knew I was gifted. Not the kind every mom says about their genus child. I knew I had an outside connection with something out of this world. I knew helping others was what I was supposed to do. Out of everything that I have been through, it's the only thing that makes sense. I've been through pain, tests, trials, tribulations and been broken just to be able to help someone else. But before I get in too deep with that, let me share this; we all have a story. What matters is how your story is told. Live in your truth. Embrace everything life throws at you. Sit the embarrassment cup down and highlight your scars. It's what made you who you are today. Always remember where you came from, but stay focused on where you're trying to go. What you're going to love most about this book is that it's relatable. We all have some sort of similarity. You are going to see some of me in you. When you do, you're going to be inspired to become a better version of yourself in one area or another.

Here's a little background of me. I was born and raised on the east side of Detroit, MI. I was born to a 38-year-old Cancer mom and a 42-year-old

Aquarius dad. I didn't grow up in a two-parent household. I never had an opportunity to ask them why did they separate. My mom had older children from a previous marriage. When I was born, my brother was 22, and my sisters were 20 and 18 years old. I am my Father's only child. I grew up in a fair middle-class neighborhood with my mom. My father's neighborhood was a bit on the poorer side than my mom's. My zodiac sign is referred to as an Aries. I'm a full-blown fire Ram. I was born on Easter Sunday, April 3rd. Now I know some of you are reading this and saying to yourself wow, "she has to be so cool!" Well, guess what? You guessed right! However, under all of my coolness, I endured so much pain, disappointment, sadness, anger, insecurities, joy, sense of humor, love, and passion.

I was born to no living grandparents. Both parents had a large number of siblings of at least 8 on each side. I only knew two of my aunts and uncles in total. Both of my parents died when I was at a young age. Both of my parents were on drugs. I was involved in a brutal home invasion. I've been raped and was told I may never be able to have children. I lost two of my best friends by the age of 12 years old. I was a teenage mom. I'm a 100% single parent of two children with no help from any family members. Not even their own fathers. I've been homeless. My child was sexually assaulted and had second-degree burns before the age of 4 years old. I was involved in a domestic violence relationship for years. My closest sister passed away. I've fought suicidal thoughts and depression. Yet, throughout all of this tragic, I still have room in my heart to encourage you! Life has its way of turning nothing into a whole lot of something. They say diamonds are formed by heat and under pressure, right? That's why I'm ready to tell my story. To know me is to love me. So, let's get to know me a little bit.

Chapter 1 - I see you in me

As I mentioned in my introductory note, my government's name is Julena, but I'm known as Juju or Ju to the world. Both are intelligent, resilience, strong, dedicated, ambitious, goal orientated, show good character, have morals, integrity, and principles. But they both can be stubborn or, as my mom used to say, "very hard headed". My name is so locked in to Juju and Ju that some people don't even know my government name, even when we've known each other for years. I have some family members who don't know my government name. I know it sounds crazy, but that's just the truth. Let me tell you the difference between the two: they're like night and day.

Julena is like my little sister, who I keep in the house. She is (in some cases) the little girl that I have to protect. She's very fragile, sensitive, scared, vulnerable, and soft. I keep her hidden from the world because she's been hurt so many times. She can be so kind, sweet, gullible, warm, shy, understanding, compassionate, and oblivious. She sees good in everybody. Sometimes, so much that it hurts her. I like to refer to her as the little girl who hasn't grown up yet. She wants to be seen and heard. She wants to be accepted and feel appreciated. She's an introvert. She enjoys being alone and unbothered. At the same time, she wants to be loved and feel worthy of anything good. She would also go on trips or dates by herself. She thinks things thorough and finds patience before taking action. She can be indecisive at times. She's an emotional thinker. She sometimes trusts too much without proof to be trusted. Her company is like a breath of fresh air. It's very calming and relaxed. Julena is very caring and forgiving. But she doesn't know her worth. That's when Juju comes in, shining like a star.

Now, my girl Ju is something different. She's fun, outgoing, adventurous, courageous, confident, protective, passionate, fearless, and funny as heck. She can also be sarcastic and extremely blunt though. Some people might even call her mean, raw, uncut, spoiled, unfiltered, or cold. She can even be a little controlling. Yet, I call her my hero. Ju takes chances. She's a risk taker. She's the one who can keep up with the crowd and has everyone having fun when people are around her. She's very social. She can pretty much adapt to any situation and get along with anyone. She is the one that doesn't give a fuck what anyone thinks of her. She lives life freely. She can be very outspoken and sometimes puts herself in dangerous situations. When she put that "I'm from the eastside of Detroit " hat on, just go ahead and get out of her way because that can go either really good or really bad. There are no in-between moods with this one. She's either at 0 or 100 on the scale chart. She doesn't trust a soul. She sees people for what they show. She doesn't try to see anything deeper or the potential of what a person can be. She likes to live in the moment. This is the one social media and the rest of the world love and see often.

Despite the two split personalities, they're in the same body. I know some of you can relate to this. You show people one side of you, but deep down, there's another side of you that you will only show when or if necessary. Little do we know, the vulnerable side is actually the stronger side. We just have to learn how to have a better understanding to be more emotionally intelligent with it. What I mean by this is if we stop thinking that if we open ourselves up too soon or too deep or to the wrong person, we will get hurt. By being emotionally intelligent, you're able to control your emotions more than your emotions control you. Even if you were to get hurt, it's okay. Just think about every heartbreak or disappointment you ever had, it pulled a different kind of strength out of you. We may not ask for this strength, but it's what we need at the time to get into our next chapter. What doesn't kill us will always make us stronger.

Pain is what helps us grow. We need pain to learn more about ourselves. Just think about it: the more pain you've been through, the more it makes you seek yourself. If you're always loving, fun, and happy, you would rarely put yourself on a discovery journey or get closer to yourself. Every time you put yourself on a self-healing path, you come out loving yourself a little more than you did before the pain. True enough, it hurts. But it's worth it. The more you are in tune with your emotions, the less hurt you will experience. It's like the saying, "you cannot get one up on me if I beat you to it first". Being emotionally intelligent takes a lot of courage and patience. But it's the only way to break the curse of so many people being guarded and lost. Have you ever heard of "hurt people hurt people'? There are so many people that haven't healed from past traumas and don't even realize it. Because certain things happened so long ago, they think that they got over it when all they did was wrap it up in a blanket and put it to the side, not realizing how cluttered their room (their brain) is. Unconsciously, we tend to think that we moved forward from things just because time has moved on. That's not always the case. Time does not heal all wounds; facing the pain does. This is where "healed people, heal people" comes in.

Have you ever heard of the phrase "there's sunshine after the rain"? Have you ever thought that there would be no sunshine without the rain? True joy is steamed from coming from something terrible. You can't really appreciate life and all the good things life has to offer without some disappointments. Don't be afraid to be vulnerable. Don't be afraid to be open. Don't be afraid to show people the little person inside of you. You'll never know what type of friendship or relationship can come from that. Some people need you to be open first. Creating a safe dialogue can help others feel safe. Not everyone wants to go see a therapist, a pastor or go to support groups. Some of us just need help acknowledging why we feel the way we do. Sometimes, we can be angry or sad out of nowhere. We could be okay one minute, and we feel a sense of mood change out of nowhere. That stems from something different than what actually got them to react the way they did. The way they reacted was the cover up to something deeper, most times, without them even realizing it. With the mood change, we tend to show it or rub that energy off on someone else. When we transfer that energy, they tend to pass it to someone else, and the chain continues. But what if we're able to catch that mood before the transfer? What if we start unpacking those wrapped-up, unanswered piles of thoughts before they affect our daily living? Doing this would start the process of converting those two people inside of you.

In order for someone to love you wholeheartedly or for you to love someone else wholeheartedly, you have to show who you are entirely. Otherwise, we're only giving a partial side of us to be accepted. When the other side shows up, people will not know how to handle that different side of you. We shorten ourselves of living a full life when we only give partial. If you're wondering how to start this new you, here are some questions to ask yourself.

1. What does love mean to you? Is it just an emotion? Is it what others can do for you?
2. What truly makes you happy? Exclude other people and materialistic things.
3. How do you connect with people? Through your words? Through actions?
4. Are you aware of what your needs are in a long-term relationship? What feeds your soul?
5. What can you give to a relationship? Outside of finances and good looks.

6. When you look in the mirror, how do you see yourself? What are some of your immediate thoughts after seeing your reflection (besides how good you look).

7. What haven't you forgiven yourself for? When was the last time you apologized to yourself?

8. What haven't you forgiven others for? Did you actually tell the person who disappointed you how they made you feel?

9. What do you love most about yourself?

10. What do you love least about yourself? Are you lazy? Angry? Bad breath?

11. What would mattered if you died yesterday? Not tomorrow. What do you wish you could swap that time for?

12. What would you congratulate your one year older self for? Speak into what is going to happen for you this year.

13. What would you tell your 5 year old self?

14. What gets you the most angry? 15. How are you making your deceased loved one proud?

These are the questions I had to ask myself. So I decided to write about it, in hopes of inspiring you!

L

Chapter 2

Faith got me through doors that fear couldn't

There are many more self-evaluating questions, but let's start there now. Asking myself some of these questions was the start of my new journey. Don't get me wrong; I was always trying to self-improve and upgrade my self-love journey for most of my adult life. I started fasting in my twenties. For those who are unfamiliar with fasting, it's when you sacrifice things that you love or feel like you can't live without for a period of time to focus on what's important to you. I've done so many fastings with and without my church. Most of the time, I don't give myself time to prepare before entering it. I just dive right in and sacrifice cold turkey whatever I think would be hard to let go or any distractions that hold me from communicating better with The Lord. On my very first fasting, I gave up beef, pork, alcohol, sweets, TV, and radio if it wasn't about God. I also gave up all personal social media. up. Giving up these things gave me time to focus on God and to pray more.

Every time I had the urge to eat a slice of pepperoni pizza or turn on my favorite reality show, I prayed instead. Cutting these things gave me extra time to focus on what was important to me. Going into a fast, I had to make what I wanted clear. Most of the time, it was to receive a clear direction from the Most High. By no means is fasting easy. As adults, we tend to move freely, doing what we want and when we want to, especially when no one is taking care of us. There is very little discipline and obedience in adult nature. Fasting over the years has taught me patience and obedience. Each time I do it, my willpower is stronger than the time it was before. Hey, I'm not trying to force religion on anyone. You can even call it something else. However, just try it one time to see how you feel. I usually sacrifice 40 days. However, you can go how long you want to. I have never done it and regretted it. Fasting has taught me to be still, listen to my consciousness, connect with my energy, trust my thoughts, and cleanse myself. Most importantly, it helps me to identify what I thought I couldn't live without, I actually can. Moving around every day and having a routine, we tend to lose ourselves and develop this "existing in this world" vs "living in this world" concept. What made me realize that change was needed was thinking about "how many summers I possibly have left". There will always be another July 25th, but it'll never be another July 25, 2023, again. I have to make this life thing count. I suffered enough, this is not what life is about. It's now up to me to live an abundant life. But to get there, I must make some changes.

I believe life is about never stop elevating and growing. Life is about having ups and downs but coming out of the downs that made us stronger. If you think about it, when was the last time you went through something and did not overcome it or did it shape you to become a superwoman/superman? Life is about continuing to move forward. Whether we like it or not, life will continue to move on with or without us. It's up to us to make the best out of it or let the worse take over us. It's okay to sit in your feelings temporarily but do not give yourself too much time to stay there. Your circumstances are for you to stand in, not let it stand on you. Believe it or not, you are not the first person to have been through whatever you're going through. Sorry to tell you that you may not be the last. I know it's something that happened to you that you didn't ask for, but just like you didn't ask for some of the good, it's just the way life is. What happened to you, also happened for you. What we have to do while we're here is make the best situation out of any situation because we are on a time clock. We're only here temporarily. Are you here to be remembered or forgotten? Speaking for myself, I'm signing up for the remembered department.

Writing this book feels very uncomfortable. I'm letting the world see my vulnerable side. I'm a very private person but at the same time I'm social. This means I have no problem with showing the world when I'm happy or having fun but if something real is going on with me, I keep it to myself. It took my therapist years to uncover a lot of my real feelings and thoughts. That's right, I have seen a therapist before. I know some people think that therapists are for crazy people but those people are the ones who have never tried it for themselves. Seeing a therapist helped me discover the core of the reasons why I think the way I think and act the way I act. Although, I was considered an adult when I first started seeing a counselor, I was still behaving immaturely, reacting out of anger before thinking, I took everything personal which led me to always be moody and unhappy, I was extremely insecure, I couldn't communicate well to others and most importantly, I didn't know how to properly grieve. Although time has gone on from losing people that were close to me, I never sat still long enough to heal from it properly. I was honestly just living life with no direction or purpose. Deep down I thought that if I sat still, pain would take over my mind and heart. I didn't want to feel that. I didn't want to cry. I didn't want to remember. I didn't want to talk about anything real. I was very comfortable with feeling numb. I thought nobody would be able to hurt me because I didn't allow them "in".

I had to start over, almost like hitting a redo button. I wanted better for myself. I just didn't know how to get it. I knew it was more to life than just suffering and not being happy. I didn't know what I wanted exactly, I just knew what I didn't want and that was to be unhappy all of my life. I questioned God a lot. I was even angry with him a couple times. The days I was alone in my dark room, I used to ask God why I was cursed. What did I do wrong to have a life like the one I had? It just wasn't fair, I said. I thought the church was for hypocrites and old people. It was even a point in my life when I was suicidal. Living was just too hard, I used to tell myself. In those moments, I used to hear my moms voice saying "if you kill yourself, you will cash in your going to heaven ticket guaranteed". If killing myself was off the table of my "todo list" I had to figure something else out because being miserable wasn't fun. I knew my life was worth more, I just had to find direction on how to get to the "worth" part.

Let's start from the beginning before I reach this point. Let's take it back to when I was about four years old.

Chapter 3

How you see me

Taking it back to some of my first memories. When I was about four years old, my mother and I lived off Dexter and Davison on Detroit's west side. I would say I was a pretty happy kid. I used to play outside like any other kid. At the apartments where we lived, my sister, Ariel, her husband at the time, and her children stayed in the same apartment complex downstairs from us. My nieces and nephews are all close in age as me. We kind of grew up like siblings. I was at their house when they weren't at grandma's house playing with me. Over the years, I would say we were all very close. Ariel has five kids in total, Terri has four in total.. My brother (we call him Pooh) does not have any biological children. He was in prison for the first 16 years of my life for armed robbery. He almost had a son who would have been the same age as me but unfortunately did not survive.

I was writing to Pooh before I learned how to write. I drew pictures to express my feelings most of the time. He said he understood what I was saying, but that was his way of protecting my feelings. We wrote letters to one another faithfully. He was my best friend. I remember being so excited to hear that collect call coming through our house phone. If it was one thing my mom taught us, it was to love each other. We were all we had, she always said. My mom, her kids, and her grandchildren were all I knew. I never missed what I didn't have. Growing up with all her grandkids as if we were all siblings never left me with a dull moment. We had so much fun together. It was a party everytime we linked up. We used to make up our own games, cook together, play nintendo or sega genesis, rehearse dance routines, go bike riding, fight and immediately make up. We knew each other's secrets. We did almost everything together. The things we didn't do together, we told each other about it. The only thing we didn't do together was I never really attended the schools that they attended. That didn't stop us from having one another back. If we needed each other for any reason, we were bringing everybody. They were truly my best friends.

Well, let me take it back. My mom had a sister named Carry. She and my aunt had a very strange relationship. Everyone said that they used to fight and argue all the time, then turn around and laugh it off. I don't remember that. I only remember that sometimes I would see them not speak when they were dropping me off or picking me up. Other times, they would be laughing and enjoying one another's company. My aunt always spoiled me and called me her favorite niece. Her daughter Elise and I were best friends. We were like salt and pepper. We were polar opposites but complemented each other perfectly. Although, my aunt had six other kids, Elise and I were inseparable. We were the same age, she was only 3 months older than me. We did everything together, from playing with our favorite toys, to arguing, to getting in trouble together, to making up our own games or playing jokes on her older siblings. Elise was unique because she was never afraid of anything. She couldn't feel pain and never cried from a feeling. If emotionless was a person, she was it. It used to amazes me that when we would get a whooping for whatever we've done wrong, she would make herself cry to make the beating stop. If my aunt recognizes that she's faking, she will go harder. Elise used to eat it up so effortlessly. After the whooping was over, she would immediately go back to normal without a single tear. To this day, I still do not know how a person cannot feel any pain. It still amazes me when I think about it.

Sometimes I remember my aunt's oldest daughter, Tania, coming to our apartment to babysit me while my mom went to work. I hated it when Tania babysat me. She was always drunk. When she had a few beers, she would chase me around the apartment with a lit cigarette. I used to tell my mom about the experiences, but she always laughed it off and said, "Your cousin will never hurt you." As a kindergartener, I didn't trust that. That lady was scary. I'm not sure how old she was. If i had to guess i would say at least 21 years old since she was always intoxicated. The rest of my Aunts' children didn't have a relationship with me growing up. Either they were too old or too young for me. I never really met any of my mom's other siblings and their kids. In fact, I didn't even know that she had other siblings until I became older.

When I was older my mom told me her parents had a bunch of kids. I asked "well where are they? Where have they been? And most importantly when did you have parents?" Her response was "my living brothers and sisters and I do not talk and your grandparents died before you were born." I said "well can we go get them from being undead and find the other people?". She then just cried. I never wanted to talk about it again.

One of my best memories at the age of 4 years old was when my mom and I did a photoshoot. At the time, I wasn't happy. I can't remember exactly why I was so unhappy. I just remember the photographer wanted me to smile, and I refused to do so, for the most part. I wanted to be stubborn and show my mother a lesson that I wanted my way. Of course, that's not what happened. My mom always knew how to cheer me up. To this day, that is one of my favorite photoshoots. I wore a black and white poke-a-dot dress and a huge bow at the top of my head. That's probably the reason why I was mad. A few years later, we took another photoshoot, but this time, my mom took some pictures with me. This is one of my favorite memories at this age because it's one of the only photos I have of my mom by ourselves. Exposing me to photoshoots at such an early age made me fall in love with the camera. Not just in front of the camera, I loved capturing the moments. I would always beg my mom for a camera to take photos of just about anything happening in the day. I'm surprised I didn't grow up to be a supermodel or photographer. My family knew they could count on me to show up with a camera everytime I came around. I always wanted to hold on to memories, capturing the moment lasted longer, I always thought. My dreams are kind of like photo memories as well.

It's certain dreams that I will never forget. Once upon a time, I prayed to God to even remove my dreams from me because of how traumatizing they are. At the age of about seven years old, while still staying on Dexter and Davison, I had a dream that my aunt Carry was on a mountain. I remember this dream as if I had it last night. There was a lot of fire coming from under the mountains. Almost like she was on top of a volcano. In my dream, she was shouting my mom's name to come help her. She would say, "Jo, Jo, come help me! Please help me! The fire is rising.!" My mom would explain, "I'm trying to get over there. One of us might have to jump over." My Aunt said, "What if one of us doesn't make it? That's too risky". My mom interrupted me in a frantic saying, "We have to go right now!" I had no idea what was going on. I later found out that night my aunt Carry was gunned down with her teenage son in the car at the local gas station. Thankfully, they didn't kill him because he played like he was shot and fell over as the shots were going off. I'm unsure what actually happened, and I was too young to understand. I don't remember it being anything like a robbery. We all think it may have been someone she knew. I just know my favorite aunt was murdered the same night I had a dream about her. Talk about freaked out! I couldn't sleep alone for a long time after that.

We moved into my aunt's house on the east side so her kids could stay together and not go to foster care. My mom and my sister Terri moved in together to take care of my aunt's oldest four children, my sister's two kids and myself. We were all one big, blended family. To this day, her murder is unsolved. My aunt's oldest children stayed at the house, but her youngest three (including Elise) moved in with their dad almost immediately. I remember my mom being so upset by that. She wanted all the kids to stay together. Because he was the biological father, my mom couldn't do anything about it. She tried her best to visit them, have them come over, and just stay in contact. But my little cousin's father always moved, changed his number, and wouldn't tell us anything. Which made it quite difficult to stay in touch with the children. About a year and a half later, I caught a random horrible feeling. It was a really bad feeling out of nowhere. Almost like a Deja Vu. Something was wrong, but I didn't know what. I later found out later that same day that my favorite cousin Elise had passed away. I was so confused. I didn't understand what these people were telling me. When I heard the words "Elise is dead", my seven-year-old self felt like someone had hit me with a bus. The pain hit hard.

Although my Aunt had just passed away, I had an idea of what death was. In my mind, she was a grown-up. I loved her, but I thought grown-ups were supposed to die. I was only seven years old. Elise and I were the same age. "How was her being dead even possible?" is all I kept asking myself. Our family was told she swallowed a balloon, and the adults couldn't get the balloon out of her airways. That was the original story. However, the story changed a few times over the years. No autopsy was done, so we don't know for sure what actually happened. My mom always questioned that story, but she couldn't prove anything otherwise. Of course, after the funeral, their father disappeared again. We couldn't find them. Back in the day, there was no such thing as Google, internet searches, smartphones, or any technology we use today to find people. We didn't even have child protected services. I remember my mom going to the police station a few times to get help, but there wasn't much she could do.

About two years after Elise's death, her little brother, Marvin, passed away. He was only four years old. Now, can you imagine how this would affect a child? Something wasn't right. I was scared. I had already been to more funerals than I wanted to. All I remember thinking was, "Is this normal?" To this day, we also don't know what happened to him. That story was also changed many times by the father over the years. I remember my mom trying to take him to court to fight for custody of the last child he had. Of course, she lost the petition because she couldn't prove he had anything to do with his children's sudden deaths. Our family knew something was not right. My aunt was violently murdered with her son in the car; almost two years later, her seven-year-old daughter mysteriously died. Two years after that, her 4-year-old son also mysteriously passed away. Of course, after that, we didn't see them again for years. It was like they disappeared off the face of the earth. When we would finally see Aaliyah, we often asked her what actually happened? You could tell she was so frightened. It's almost like she would immediately go into shock mode. Her face became blank and she would rock back and forth. It was clear that she was traumatized. Sometimes, she would answer us with a different answer than she gave to someone else. Other times she would simply say "I'm not allowed to talk about it".

Chapter 4
You have to know the beginning to understand the end

Being closer to my dad was more important to me than ever after. When we moved to the east side, I could see my dad more often. I was his only child, so when I visited him, I was at peace and quiet paradise. Back with my mom, there were just too many kids at home. We had to share rooms and see each other every single day. I didn't like that. I was used to being alone and having my own space. If any kids came to visit, they would eventually go home after a while. I liked having company but also enjoyed playing alone and having my freedom. When I visited my dad at his apartment on East Warren, it was my happy time. My dad always spoiled me. I rarely heard the word "no " with him. I never received a whooping, no matter how upset I made him. He always threatened to, though. Even him being angry at me was enough to correct my behavior. I looked at my dad as this big, awesome, superior guy. In my eyes, he was a king and I was his princess. His words meant everything, and making him proud meant the world to me. When I visited him, we would watch the Simpsons or sports games like basketball, football, boxing, or wrestling. They were our favorite programs. After our shows, I would go into my room and watch my own shows, such as Sister, Sister, and Moesha. Then I would put my favorite cassette tape in my cassette player and play with my Barbies and Barbie Dream House on his patio. I had the whole collection of barbies. I had all the clothes, two dream houses, 3 dream cars and many Barbie dolls. When I wasn't playing with my Barbies, I would play my dad in card games, dominoes, checkers, or board games. He kept his radio station on 98.7 (back then, that was the jazz station). He would have me stand on his feet while we ballroom around our living room. He often would take me for a walk and talk to get some fresh air and spend some quality time outside of the apartment. Sometimes, he would have me braid his hair knowing I didn't know what I was doing, but he said, "Practice makes perfect," so I kept trying.

Although I loved visiting my dad, we were poor. My dad's apartment was very clean but it was infested with roaches and mice. I know it sounds contradicting but it's true. He was a big neat freak. Everything had to be perfectly in place and he cleaned and wiped down every single day. But that didn't stop the infestation. Many times, I was so afraid to walk on the floors because of the mice. You could hear them talking and running around all night long. It was like when the lights went down, a party was had. They were often so loud. I was terrified to go to sleep alone. If my dad wouldn't allow me to sleep with him, I would sleep with my headphones on and music playing to shut the noise out. If I had to use the restroom I would try my best to hold it in until the morning. But if i couldn't make it, I would rather either pee in the bed or grab a cup on the nightstand to use and empty it the next morning. The roaches were everywhere. They were different from the mice. They never waited for the lights to go down to show up. They came out whenever they wanted to. The pregnant ones were the worst. It was almost like you didn't want to kill them, being pregnant and all, but the eggs hanging on the back of them were so fat and disgusting you had to kill them and any family members that came to try to rescue them. They were a real family. It was almost like the more you kill them, the more they multiply.

We didn't have a washing machine so we either had to wash our clothes with our hands in the tub or sink or take them to his sister's house if she would be kind enough to allow us to do our laundry in her basement. Sometimes, we would have hot water without cold or cold without hot. My dad rarely had food in the fridge or cabinets. We used to have to eat at the soup kitchen with the other low-income families and homeless people. I was so embarrassed when we went. I sometimes didn't even eat because I was so embarrassed. I would say to myself, "I would rather starve than eat with these people". Sometimes, when I would visit my dad, he would take me to his sister's house for meals because he knew how I felt about the soup kitchen. I sometimes loved visiting my Aunt's because my little cousins were always there. There were four of us: Tasha, Lonna, Nikki and me. Lonna and Nikki were close, and Tasha and I were close. Although we all were close collectively, we somehow broke into alliances. Lonna and Nikki were younger, and Tasha and I were the older cousins. We are all two years apart from one another. In my opinion, the grownups treated the younger ones better. It was definitely some favoritism being played. Lonna and Nikki snitched on everything Tasha and I did.

They were the two younger cousins who were spoiled, whining, and goodie two shoes. Goodie, two shoes means that they did no wrong in their own eyes. They did everything by the book. They were so annoying sometimes because I liked to bend the rules. The rules were extremely strict. We basically couldn't do anything besides sit on the porch or go in the yard to get on the swing set or watch tv but we had to stay in the living room and watch whatever the adults were watching (which mostly was the old people stories or the news). We weren't allowed to listen to the FM station which played r&b and hip hop music. We were only allowed to listen to gospel music. Nikki, Tasha, and Lonna were all my aunts' grandchildren. I was her only niece who came around. This was the only family that I knew on my paternal side. I was told that my father had more family somewhere down south, but he didn't talk to them, and we never visited them. To this very day, I still don't know them and don't think that I ever met them.

When I wasn't playing with my cousins at my aunt Ruth's house, I'd be at my dad's house in my zone. I would go outside from time to time to play with the neighborhood kids. My dad often wouldn't allow me to leave the side of the street where his apartment was located. I wanted to go across the street where the cool kids were. Sometimes, he would allow me to go across the street and be back when the streetlights came on. For some reason, it seemed like those streetlights came on as soon as I stepped outside. Just as soon as we were having fun, the lights would come on and I would have to rush home. If I disobeyed my dad, he would be so disappointed in me and my punishment would always be I couldn't either go outside the next day or I couldn't leave the street if I did, which both sucked. I was such a tomboy (a little boy trapped inside a girl's body) when it came to outside. I wanted to play football and street basketball, ride rough bikes with the boys, play video games, and box. That used to be the time of my life. I got along with almost everyone. Although my parents didn't have a lot of money, they kept me dressed very nicely. I always had what others had. Not just my wardrobe was kept up, my parents kept me nice all the way around. I didn't even know I was poor until I became an adult. My parents kept me in the finest jewelry (real gold and diamonds). I had a laptop, new bikes, a typewriter and a phone. It sounds small but back then this was a big deal. Although I didn't always eat what I wanted, I never missed a meal.

Kids at school and some of the neighborhood kids would make fun of my dad for being older. As I said, he was already 42 years old when I was born. This used to get me furious. They talked about other stuff as well, such as we lived in raggedy apartments, we didn't have a running car, my dad was dark, I smelled bad, I was tall, skinny, I had a gap in my top row teeth and said that I had a booty nose. Throughout everything they said, talking about my dad always got me ready to fight. None of that other stuff really got to me. One day, a girl from the neighborhood and I were playing with our dolls, and she started bad-mouthing my dad. She was asking why my dad have roaches, why we were so broke, why didn't my dad have a car, why my dad was so old and black and so on. I stood up and said, "My dad has a lot of money. He has so much money he can buy me anything I want! Can you say the same?". Now, I don't remember what happened after that, but I do know that shortly afterwards, we were involved in a home invasion.

I can't remember if it was the same night, but I do remember the burglary happening almost immediately. When I was awakened out of my sleep, a gun was pointed at the temple of my face. My daddy was in front of me, bleeding out from what appeared everywhere. I have never been more scared in my life. So much blood was leaking from my father's head. One man had a gun to my head, saying, "If you don't tell us where the money is, we will blow her head off, do not tempt us." The other man was beating my daddy with the back of his gun, dragging him by his hair, screaming, "Tell us where the money is now!" These men were tall and medium build, dressed in all black and wearing ski masks. I remember every detail as if it happened yesterday. If I heard the voice to this day I'm almost sure I can identify it. My daddy looked at me and said, "It's in the coat closet in the living room in a crown royal purple bag." while spitting blood up. The man hit him again across the head. My dad fell unconscious, bleeding out. The man who had the gun to my head looked me in my eyes and said, "Stay here! Do not move or I will come back. You don't want me to come back do you?." I want to say I urinated on myself and shook my head "no".

Once I felt that they were gone, I kept trying to wake my daddy up, but he wouldn't wake up. I ran to our house phone and called my Aunty and dialed 911 immediately afterwards. Ruth lived about 3 minutes away. I was so young, but I memorized her number. In fact, I believe that's the only number that I knew at the time. Growing up, she told me that's one of the reasons she never changed her number was because of this night. She wanted everybody to be able to call her if they needed her. Ruth and dad both always reminded me that I was the cause of that robbery. I carried that with me every day. The amount of guilt I had was weighing me down. This near-death experience has taught me so many lessons. One main lesson was to stop talking so much. Nobody needs to know your business, especially in your household. I don't care if people think you only have two quarters to your name. Let them think whatever they want. It's none of their business. I also learned that everybody isn't your friend. They will smile in your face and set you up the moment you turn your back.

My mom used to always say, "Keep your friends close but your enemies closer." This incident also taught me to always have protection and an emergency plan. I always have to be prepared for the worst. I learned that it's okay for people to have their opinions of you. It's not your job to change the way they look at you. Most importantly, I learned not to share anyone else's business with anyone. No matter how mad I am at someone, you can't pay me to share a secret of theirs. Maybe that's why it was so hard for me to trust people growing up. The memories of this still haunt me. From that day forward, my daddy never slept in bed again. He always slept on the couch in the living room with a gun and other guns in secret spots. He taught me that they were for safety precautions and the purpose of them is for protection. I wasn't afraid of being around guns because both of my parents taught me at a young age that as long as it is used for protection, I don't have to be afraid of them. He put extra locks and boards on the doors. He also never went into a deep sleep. He wasn't much of a deep sleeper anyway because he's a Vietnam vet.

He was drafted into the military at the age of 18 years old. I loved hearing about the stories of when he was enlisted in the army. He was indeed my hero. He was honorably discharged because he was shot in the leg. His position was a paratrooper. During the Vietnam war, they were drafting many colored males to the army. If you refuse to join, you will receive jail time. He was from the south born in the 1940's, so racism was very much alive. He told me stories about how some of his close friends would be killed right in front of him. They would be walking and having a conversation, and the person he was talking to would walk in front of a landmine and blow up right before his eyes. This can leave a person traumatized as imagined. He told me so many terrifying stories, you would think I would never want to enlist in the army. When, in fact, it made me want to go. I wanted to be a hero like my father. I believe he protected his friends, our freedom, and the whole country. In my opinion, that was incredible.

The army had to pay him for the rest of his life. Any children he had received benefits, too. I was born nearly 20 years after his discharge and I was receiving benefits. How cool was that? He made me promise him to never join the army. He said, "I didn't have a choice, but you do. So don't do it." The nightmares and being a survivor (if you even survive) aren't worth it. I did it so you wouldn't have to." That always stuck with me. After leaving the military, he moved to Detroit, Michigan from Dublin, Georgia, where he was born and raised with his sister Ruth. Together, they created a new life away from their parents, other siblings and the rest of their family. He then started working at the Chrysler Motor plant. Landing a job at one of the big three was a big deal back in the day. There were so many people moving from all around the world to work at the Detroit motor companies. Unfortunately, some object blew up in my father's face, which caused him to become disabled from Chrysler and working all together. That was the last job he ever had. Chrysler had to pay him for the rest of his life behind that.

Chapter 5
Change atmospheres

As a result of the robbery, my mom did not let me see my dad for what felt like years. She blamed him for it and said I wasn't safe with him. That crushed my soul. I loved and missed my dad every day. I was mad at my mom for a long time after that. She would always say, "I know what's best for you, and until you have kids, you won't understand!". Not long after the incident with my dad, my mom's house was broken into. This one wasn't as bad or violent though. I remember all the kids were sleeping in the living room. I kept hearing noises from the back door, but I was too scared to get up to check it out. Moments later, I saw men wearing all black walking through the house. I closed my eyes and pretended to be asleep. That was when I peed on myself again. I was a big bedwetter after these situations. It is very rare that I'll be asleep when I wet the bed. I used to be wide awake, peeing on myself because I was always too afraid to use the bathroom while everyone was asleep. Those robbers came and took whatever they wanted and left. When everyone else woke up, I told them all what happened. After the incident, my mom bought guns, and my sister bought pitbull dogs. These dogs never stopped barking, and this is why.

We had spirits (some people call them ghosts) living in the house. Now, you're probably wondering, "Yep, she's crazy for sure". But I assure you that spirits do exist in this world. All of my nieces, nephews and I used to have these weird feelings like someone was looking at us when we were in an empty room. We used to hear certain things at different times. Doors would shut on their own. I saw shadows through the mirrors. lights and tv's would turn on and off by themselves. I saw shadows a few times with my own eyes. No one else could see them. They only heard or felt them. They were so fast! They would do some evil things. One day, my nieces and I were playing upstairs on the second floor of our home. As we were running around playing tag, only one of my nieces and I were the last to leave upstairs. So, we started running towards the stairs to go back downstairs. My niece was in front of me, closer to the staircase than I was. A spirit looked at me, smiled, and pushed her down the stairs. I screamed, "Watch out!" Before she was able to stop running to figure out what I was screaming about, she was pushed. She rolled down the stairs and she hit her head on a car battery that was sitting at the end of the staircase. Our mom's had to rush her to the hospital. At first, they blamed me for it. But our stories matched. There was no way for me to have pushed her. I was too far away. She told them she felt someone pushed her and that I was located on the other side of the room where the bed was. We told our moms about the spirits before this incident, but they never believed us. I think they believed us at this point because we moved out shortly afterwards.

Not long later, we all moved out of the spooky house. My cousins ended up staying with my sisters temporarily, and my mom and I moved in with my dad. Man, I was the happiest kid on earth! My mom enrolled me in a school opposite from the neighborhood kids school but I was still happy. We were all under one roof. My parents would take turns walking me to school and picking me up every day. There were days I would say "I'm a big girl and can walk by myself." They were not having that. I could never walk with my friends or by myself home. My favorite memory with my parents is when we took a family photo with Santa at my elementary school. To this day, that's the only photo I have of all of us together. They told me to sit on Santa's lap, so I did and started acting silly. I was pissing my mom off. She wanted the picture to be perfect, but I refused to cooperate. We ended up settling for me, making a slightly funny face. Looking back at that moment, I wish I had cooperated better if I knew we would never get that opportunity again.

Living with both parents was so much fun. I've finally felt what my friends were experiencing having my home complete. My dad protected me when I got in trouble with my mom. My mom styled my hair almost every other day. They took turns cooking meals every night. It was rumored that my Aunt didn't like my mom much, so we didn't visit her house that often. My mom didn't like the soup kitchens either, so that was also canceled. I was so happy. I had everything I ever wanted. They had me taking piano lessons with the man downstairs in our apartment building. I hated it because he smelled so bad. It smelled like he never took a bath in his life and he pissed himself every night. The smell was so bad you could smell it outside of the apartment building because his apartment was only on the second floor. The smell used to make my eyes water and clog my nose up. I didn't understand why I had to play piano. My dad would say it's more than just the piano, he has wisdom. Always take advantage of the wisdom the elders have to offer. In my mind, this man had to be at least 200 years old. Whatever he had to offer was old news, I thought. This is a new day and new time. Although his stories were interesting, my young mind couldn't conceal what he was saying to me. He was talking about plantations, civil war and slavery. Sometimes it was going in one ear and out of the other. I just knew he smelled so bad and needed a bath. After every lesson, he would give me money to go to the corner store. I was always a saver. I never spent all of my money at once. If he gave me $5, I would spend $2 and save the rest. I loved having a stash. I used to think I could buy me and my family meals if we ever had to go to the soup kitchen again. So, I continued to deal with the smell as if I were working a job. Well, that was until the man died. I was so heartbroken. Not because he died but because now, how was I going to provide for my family? I know that sounds awful, but those were the thoughts of a 4th grader. Looking back now, I wish I listened to him more.

Eventually, we moved out of my dad's apartment and into our new 3-bedroom home on Goulburn and 6 mile. My mom was officially a homeowner. She was so proud of herself. We were still on the east side but kind of far from where my dad lived. Our neighborhood was a bit nicer. When we first moved in, I was so happy that I could have two rooms all to myself. I can have a playroom and a bedroom. However, I never slept in my own room. I always needed to sleep with someone. Most people didn't like me sleeping with them because I was a bedwetter. I didn't care, I was climbing in bed with someone. Sleeping alone was never an option. Now that we're in our new home, my cousins ended up moving with us. They were older in high school, so we didn't have much in common. They thought I was too young to be around them so I always slept with my mom. I just knew they didn't like me much because their younger sister and I used to always get them in trouble. We didn't speak much about her, their brother, or my Aunt Carry. It was kind of one of those things that we just never talked about. We just pretended their deaths never happened.

Back then, seeing a counselor or therapist was for crazy people. We went to church. My mom found us a church home just a few streets over. We would walk there almost every night (or that's what it felt like). We would go to bible study, praise, and worship, and another bible study; it seemed like we were at church almost every day. Sometimes, I didn't mind because I had friends there. We had our fun while the grownups were catching the holy ghost and 'getting a word" is what they called it. I remember us always in church, but my mom was a thug immediately afterwards. She would play Tupac music all day long and would curse you out using every curse word to mankind. I remember a time she cut her sought-off gun down because it was too long to hide under her raincoat. Whenever my sisters had domestic problems with their boyfriends, they would call mommy. Mommy would show up locked and loaded, standing 10 toes down. The streets called her "crazy jo". She was one of those women you didn't want to fuck with. You'll never see her coming your way.

Don't get me wrong, my mom would give you the shirt off her back if she sees you're cold. She was a very family-oriented, loving and giving person. I saw her give and look out for people while she went without. We didn't have much family, but the ones she called family could get anything from her. She always made a way out of no way. From what I can remember, she hadn't had a job since before my Aunt was murdered. I'm not sure how she kept food on the table, a roof over our head, we had a brand-new van, clothes on my back, and the nerve to supply my wants, too. I didn't have designer things, but I always had jewelry, nice clothes, nice toys, a backyard, a house, a car, and a wagon. All of the kids on the street wanted to play in my backyard.

But the house was spooky. I think either the spirits followed up from the last house, or these were brand-new ones. I remember using the restroom and seeing a shadow under the door, walking past a few times and then eventually stopping at the door. Our door had a keyhole, so it was visible to see on the other side of the door. When I noticed that the shadow stopped at the door, I looked at the peeping hole and saw an eye look at me and blink. I felt like I had died at that moment because I was in the house alone. After the shadow walked towards the rooms in the back, I got some courage to get off the toilet and run outside in the opposite direction of the house, screaming as loud as I could for help. I ran to where my niece was playing at her friend's house, screaming at her, hoping she would say she was the one behind this. She was so confused as to what I was talking about, and her friend confirmed that they never left the porch. So, we all walked back to my house to see what or who could've been looking at me. I knew it wasn't an actual person because I remember not hearing footsteps as the shadow went back and forth, and all the doors were locked. My niece then looked at me and said, "That must have been the same spirit that tried to pull my sister under the bed."

When she first told this story, I admit I didn't believe her. She stated that she and her baby sister were on the bed watching The goosebumps show. While watching the show, her baby sister was around 3 years old at the time. She had her legs hanging from the bed, drinking out of her sippy cup. Something under the bed began to pull one of her legs down and pull her under the bed. My first thought was that the show had you locked in a crazy imagination. She said she got off the bed to pull her sister's arm to pull her from under the bed, but something under the bed was extremely strong. The baby was crying and afraid. Eventually, she was able to pull her sister from under the bed. Ironically, the same room where she said this took place was the same direction the shadow went. From that moment forward, my nieces and cousins almost never fought each other again. Sometimes we would get into these petty arguments over just about anything. When one of us had a disagreement, we would at least take it up outside or let it go. When we were inside the house, we had to always stick together and have each other's back. The adults never believed us. We all had different stories of experiences with these spirits. So, it had to be real, right?

When my nieces weren't over, I played with the neighborhood kids. I had a best friend named Issa. Issa and I have been friends since kindergarten. We went to the same school where I was living with my dad. Fate somehow put us on the same street when my mom bought our home, so we also attended the same school there. I was in the 4th grade when Issa decided that she didn't want to be my friend anymore. Around this time, I was missing a lot of school. My mom had become ill. She needed me to stay home for some days to care for her. We were on welfare, receiving food stamps, and eating boxed food from low-income facilities. My Christmas gifts came from the Good-fella (for low income home families). When you get a Good-fella box, everyone in school knows about it because they packed the boxes with the exact same items. We started eating at soup kitchens from time to time. Everyday she had me get her an orange faygo soda and a pack of cigarettes (back then any age can purchase this). Some days I had to assist her with walking, using the bathroom, giving her medications on time, cooking for her, dressing her and helping with her doctor's appointments. She had really bad days but she also had really good days.

When I finally returned to school, I didn't know a lot of the material, so I fell behind big time. Missing one day of school was like missing a week. Imagine missing weeks. On top of me being called dumb because I missed so much school, my mom couldn't do my hair like she used to. I had to style my own hairstyles. You can only imagine how that would look. I also had to dress myself. The way my mom dressed me and the way I dressed myself was completely different. My clothes didn't match, sometimes I over wore my favorite outfits and my shoes didn't match my clothes. I was going to school looking like I was taking care of myself because I was. The kids were so cruel to me. They began to bully me. The kids on my street didn't want to play with me anymore. They told Issa she had to make a choice to be their friend or mine. She chose to be their friend. They said "in order to play with us, you have to beat Julena up."

This broke my heart. I could tell she didn't really want to fight me because she prolonged it. Issa had already had 2-3 fights already. I have never fought a real fight with anyone besides my nieces when we got into disagreements. I was scared to fight someone else, let alone my best friend. I hid and ran for as long as I could to avoid this confrontation. I asked Issa one day in school, "It's okay if you don't want to be my friend, but why do you have to fight me? She responded, "I have to, but I'm not going to hurt you." Tears instantly filled my eyes. That day, I ran home to finally tell my mom what was going on. She told me, "Being bullied doesn't run in our veins." She said, "If she wants to fight, then you initiate it. One day, catch her alone walking to the store or coming home from school and fight her." She went on to say, "If you don't win, you're going to have to deal with me when I get back home." That was enough to swallow my fear and handle my business. On the next day, instead of running home from school, I walked in hopes that I would run into Issa and her friends. My hopes came into reality. The group approached me, but little did they know I was ready for them. I dropped my backpack and started whooping Issa's ass. All I was thinking was that if I don't win, I have another ass-whooping waiting at home. I have to win, I thought. I was doing a great job until her friends jumped in. Before I knew it, I had punches and kicks coming from every direction. My hair was long down the middle of my back. They were pulling my hair in so many directions I was confused as to who was doing what.

After the fight, I immediately ran home and told my mom. She immediately got up off the couch and ran outside to (in hopes) find the kids who jumped me. There wasn't a kid in sight, so she started knocking on the doors. She explained to each parent who answered their door that their child was involved in jumping me. She declared either an apology or a one-on-one fight with me and their child. The parents made their child apologize to me, but things were never the same. After that day, I pictured fighting Issa again in my head like clock work. I was almost obsessed with it. Every time I came outside, I heard kids yelling, "That's why you got beat up," and laughing with one another. They mostly were always in groups. They were never alone, so it was hard to retaliate. This led me to play only with the girl next door, who was special. She was a homeschooled kid. She couldn't close her mouth (ever), drool was always running out the side of her face, and she couldn't speak full sentences. She wanted to watch "Pretty Woman" every time we hung out. She was my only friend until my nieces and nephews came over to play with me. Her parents always thought it wasn't a good idea for her to play with other kids she didn't know. I loved her dearly and wish I could've done more to help her. Being around her helped me realize that I wanted to help others when I grew up.

Chapter 6
The nightmare that still haunts me

Besides the drama that was going on with the neighborhood kids, let me explain why I was the target of being bullied. My mom discovered that she was HIV positive and became very ill. I'm not entirely sure how she contracted the virus because I was too young for her to explain it to me. She only told me she had it. Other adult members of the family told me that she contracted it from her ex-boyfriend. Mom didn't bring home many boyfriends, so I'm not sure which boyfriend they were referring to. There was only one boyfriend I ever knew about. His name was Jacob. Jacob came around long after my mom had the virus. It's still unconfirmed whether or not he had it, but he was around for a long time. I loved and respected Jacob. He was always so nice to me. Whenever he came around, my mom was always happy. She was one of his top priorities. You can tell by the way he treated us. Even as a young child, I saw how a man is supposed to treat a lady. He was there for my mom for the good, bad and between. He didn't live with us, but he was around to help out often. There were days when my mom couldn't get out of bed or didn't eat. The only strength she had was to cry some days. When she was first diagnosed, the Doctor told her she would only live for about 6 months.

As you can imagine, that must've been extremely tough to handle. I didn't fully understand what was going on, I just knew our lives were changing before my eyes. She taught me how to drive when I was only in the 4th grade. She taught me the importance of being independent in case there ever was a day she wasn't around. I learned how to cook, do laundry, deep clean and organize. Although I wasn't in school much, she told me how important education was. She instilled in me the importance of maintaining a relationship with God no matter how hard life gets. She said life may become hard for me and I may feel like life isn't fair. She said I'm allowed to be mad at God sometimes but never to lose faith in the power of the name. Even on the days she didn't have the strength to attend church, she sent me walking those few streets to catch a word and pay her tithes. I was all she had to depend on. I remember her always telling my brother that he had to come home soon because she may not have much time left. He was the only person she trusted to continue raising me.

Not long after the diagnosis, her Aunt (the woman who raised her who she referred to as her mom) had passed away. She lived in Cincinnati Ohio. I spoke to her often, but I only remember meeting her a couple of times. I loved her dearly because my mom loved her dearly. She absolutely adored and respected her so much, you could just feel the love in their conversations. I believe that was the only person my mom had a relationship with in her family outside of her children. When she passed away, her death took my mom into a different world. There were so many days she was depressed and angry. I think she transferred a lot of that energy onto me. I remember being such a sad kid around this time. She would verbally abuse me, call me names, physically abuse me, tear my spirit down, and overall take that happy kid spirit I once had to a sad and depressed kid who felt I wasn't worth much. I used to personalize this experience all the way up until my adult years. I wasn't aware of how alone she must've felt. She's been through so much. A lot of her siblings were murdered, the ones alive weren't close to her, she was married and with a child by 16 years old, her husband was abusive and a cheater, she's been kidnapped, beaten and raped, her biological parents gave her to her aunt to be raised, her soulmate was killed (she never got over that), both her parents died, she was a single parent and so much more. She carried so much pain. So naturally, I was the closest to her and felt the backlash. In many ways, I believe she paid the price, so I wouldn't have to relive much of what she went through. She shared a lot with me at such a young age. Because of what I've witnessed and the stories she has told me, there are certain things that I would not do and there's plenty of things I do with extreme caution.

After her Aunt died, she turned to drugs. Crack cocaine, to be exact. From what I was told later in my life, that's not when she originally started doing drugs. Some people said she started using it years before I was born. But got cleaned up because she lost me to the foster care system when I was 2 years old. I cannot speak about this because I don't remember or know much about it. I don't even know if she used it while being pregnant with me. All I know is that the use of the pipe started after her Aunt (mom) died. I believe this was when she started giving up on life. She was angry at the whole world. I remember her being so mean to Jacob, but he kept coming around to check on us. She would leave me alone in the house for long periods of time. I really had to become a chef at this time, or I wouldn't eat. I had to always style my own hair. She would still buy me nice things but eventually steal them back and say someone else did it. I was one of the kids on the street to have the first everything. She spoiled me with a brand-new computer, a huge TV, a 10-speed bike with bars on the side, shiny jewelry, a Nintendo and saga genesis video game system (back then, this was our PlayStation and Xbox). Slowly but surely, it was all taken away just as soon as I got it almost. I would always go along with her lie and pretend I didn't know she was taking these things from me.

Although she was taken from me, she would never let anyone else do anything to harm me. She was overprotective of me. One day, a friend of hers name Kim was living at our home for a short period of time. I remember falling asleep on the couch and waking up to my jewelry being removed from my neck. I knew it was removed because I had that necklace for years. It never came off. I instantly told my mom. I know she wouldn't have stolen this one particular necklace from me. I can't remember the meaning behind it, but that was one thing that was off limits. I remember her calmly saying "I'll take care of it" when I told her. I didn't know what that meant at the time, I was just hurt that my special necklace was gone. A Few days later, mom came home with blood all over her and my necklace. Imagine how scared I was. She sat me down and said, "I got your necklace back, baby, put it on!" while smiling. I had to ask, "How did you get it back?" In a scared tone. She responded back, "I saw Kim at the bus stop; she usually hangs around, so I pulled up on her and shanked her." "Shanked? What's that?" I asked. She went on to say, "I stabbed her, but she's ok." I want to say that was when I pissed on myself again. I was terrified. I only kept thinking, "Who is this lady?".

From that day forward, I was too terrified to do anything to disobey her. Whatever she said, I did it within a speeding light. She's done some crazy things, like threatening my sister's boyfriends with her guns. For example, she heard my sister Terri's boyfriend had done something really horrible to my sister, so she walked to his house, knocked on his door, put a gun to his face, schooled him on how to respect a lady, and then walked off. On our way (walking) back home, she told me to hold the gun under my coat, saying if the police came, they wouldn't take me to jail. I didn't know if I respected her or was scared of her more. Deep down, I knew she would never hurt me, she loved me. I just knew something wasn't right. Maybe she did all of those crazy things because the doctor gave her a death sentence. I'm not sure. What I do know is that the sweet lady I once knew wasn't so sweet anymore.

What I appreciated the most from my mom was that she instilled in me independence, strength, drive, how important respect is to be given and to be received, and most importantly, being God fearing. She also taught me that life will not always be what I want, but I have to play with the cards I was dealt, or I'll lose. She said if I didn't learn how to play anything else, I would need to learn how to play chess. Chess would keep me thinking. The brain is the most important of all the muscles in my body. I need to always exercise. She told me to hang integrity, morals, and principles around my neck as if they were chains. She said I should view her mistakes and bad decisions as lessons, not a road map to repeat. She was preparing me for life in case she wouldn't be around. So far as you can see, before I turned the age of 10, life was lifing (as this younger generation would say).

Moving forward, the doctors were wrong. She lived longer than 6 months, but it was a rollercoaster. Going into middle school, I barely made it in. By this time, I had missed a lot of my fourth-grade year and most of my 5th grade year. In fact, I have very little memory of attending school at all during these 2 years. I remember my mom explaining to the teachers the situation with her and how much she needed me at home. I was given take-home packets to be completed weekly. I guess you can say I was home-schooled. However, no one was teaching me the learning material. I had to figure out everything on my own. Again, we didn't have the internet technology we have today, so it was much harder trying to figure out assignments. Honestly, I don't know how my teachers passed me to the next grade. In my 6th grade year, we had to move out of our home. We fell behind on our mortgage payments and our basement was flooded from a bad storm or tornado. As a result of this, the bank took our home.

I ended up moving back with my dad. My mom found a one-bedroom apartment on Houston-Whitter and Charmers, still on Detroit's east side. Back living with my dad, I started middle school, attending Barber Magnet Middle. This is a new school in a new district, so I thought meeting new friends would be a breeze. At first, it was, but that quickly ended when a student named Brenda thought it was ok to bully me because of the clothes I wore and the hairstyles I did myself. When she started roasting me (another terminology for making fun of someone), everyone thought it was okay.

What hurts about this is she used to do it in front of a boy I liked. I was always so embarrassed when everyone made fun of my skin complexion and my tall and slim shaped body. I was 5'7 and weighed about 115lbs. My hair was down my back, but I wasn't a hairstylist. My hairstyles weren't always the greatest. They talked about my teeth, my feet, my ears, my nose. The worst part of it all was that they always called me stupid because I didn't know certain school materials. They didn't know I skipped almost two grades because I cared for my sick mom at home.

One day, Brenda picked a day to actually sneak up on me. I had no idea she wanted to even fight me. She pulled my long ponytail back as I walked up the staircase so I would fall down the stairs. Once I fell, she climbed on top of me and wouldn't stop hitting me. This took me by complete surprise because, as I stated, I didn't even know we had an appointment to fight. It felt like the whole school watched the fight. I was so embarrassed. After that day, bullying me was always easy. Every day, someone made it their job to remind me of the fight. She walked around the school as if she owned it after that fight. I knew I had to get her back. I'm not entirely sure how long I waited, but I ended up arranging a meeting with her to fight again. I didn't want to do how she did it. I wanted her to know I was coming so it would be a fair chance to earn the credit. She agreed to meet me on the side of the building after school. When she walked up to me, I immediately beat her ass. After banging her head on the building, someone broke the fight up. They said I was going to kill her. I must've blacked out because I didn't even realize at the time what I was actually doing. All I felt was anger. After the fight, I ran home to my daddy. When I went home, I poured out and told him everything that had been going on. The school had already called him and instructed that a parent-teacher conference was needed the next day. Before I'd be allowed to attend that school again, I had to at least take a week off before they gave me a decision on whether or not I could come back. My mother and father attended the 2nd conference a week later. The school decided to kick me out. They stated, "Due to the severity of the fight and to protect their other students, I can no longer attend their school." I wasn't able to say goodbye to my friends or my teachers. I felt cheated.

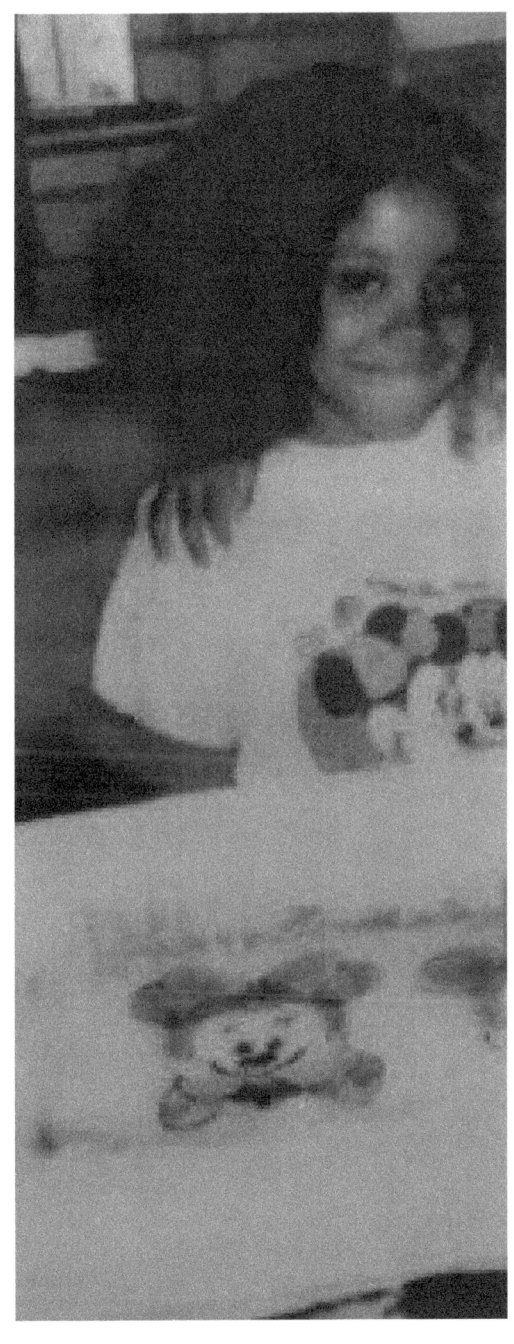

Chapter 7
What do you do when you can't do anything?

Leaving Barber Magnet Middle, I started attending Ronald McNair (formerly known as Jackson) Middle School. I had to have a whole "new start" over again. I've always been a shy person. I usually stayed to myself. While most kids were in groups or they were hanging with the popular kids, I enjoyed being alone or interacting with a selected few. I was viewed as an introvert so people used to try to test me. When this happened, other kids would stand up for me. Although I had those couple of fights in the past, I never wanted to fight again. I hated confrontation and I hated attention. I loved the sport of boxing, but I hated real life fighting. I tried to avoid them as much as I could, especially since my last fight resulted in her having to be rushed to the hospital and me getting kicked out. This school was different though. Kids were having sex, skipping school, getting pregnant, getting high, cursing in front of the teachers, driving, not listening to teachers and bragging about all of their wrongdoings to others. Not caring what anyone thinks of it. These kids were grown but trapped inside of kid bodies.

I ended up befriending a few people when I first arrived at the new school. One in particular stood out from the others. She was a white girl named Erica. She was so kind and cheerful most days. It seemed like she loved to come to school. She was one of those kids that didn't want to leave and always wanted to be there. Sometimes, the kids would down talk bad about us both if they ever saw us hanging out together. Erica was a very sensitive person. Although she was happy most of the time, she allowed a lot of stuff to make her sad or cry. I used to tell her not to let people get to her so much. There weren't many white people in our school. It was a majority black school. I used to always try to cheer her up when she often felt bad. Sometimes it worked, sometimes it didn't. Randomly, one day she told me that her stepdad was molesting her at home. This explained why she was always so quick to cry if someone said bad things to her. She told me that he made her do a lot of inappropriate things to him and he took turns doing things to her. She said she had other siblings but he only abused her. She said every time her mom would leave the house, he used her body to his disposal. She was only in the 7th grade at the time. She said it had been going on for some years. She said she told her mom, but her mom didn't believe her and refused to leave him. She said her mom never tried to even hear everything she tried to tell her. She would just cut her off mid-sentence and tell her to "stop it" and change the subject. She said after the first couple of times of trying to tell her mom about the abuse, she just stopped and dealt with it. I want to say my heart shattered into a million pieces. I felt awful. I wanted her to move in with me and my family. I felt so helpless.

I ended up telling my parents what she told me after I promised I wouldn't tell anyone, but I had to say something. I couldn't just sit around and do nothing while my friend was being abused. While I was safe in my cozy bed every night, she was home being raped and violated. That just didn't sit well with me. Now, I'm not entirely sure if my parents reported it or not. All I know is shortly after that, the school found out that she died. They said she committed suicide in the upstairs attic of her home. They said she hung herself. I think it was then that my spirit couldn't take another loss. That broke me for a long time. I don't think I ever believed that story. Although she was unhappy, she showed a lot of hope, ambition and was cheerful. Maybe this was her cover up for being in so much pain. I saw no signs that she would actually kill herself. Or maybe that's what I kept telling myself. I always blamed her mother's husband for this. There were so many nights my

12-year-old self wanted to get revenge for her death. "How could we walk the same earth with people like this?" I thought to myself. I wished bad for her mom as well. I thought to myself, what kind of mom is made aware that something may be going on with your husband and daughter and still leaves her with them? I dreamt of the day when I grew up to see them again. Sadly, I have no idea who those people are now. I still to this day, think about my friend and wonder what her life would have been like if she was still here. I think about why did it take so long for child protective service to be a thing. Would that potentially have saved her?

This time, I stayed with my dad until the ending of my sixth-grade year. I ended up moving back with my mom right before the seventh-grade summer season due to the lack of transportation to get me back and forth from school. My dad didn't like me on the public transportation and I was out of district for the school bus transportation. Living with my mom made things much easier because I was in the school bus district for my school near her apartments. I continued going to the same school for the remainder of my middle school years, which was great. I was tired of switching schools. Moving back with my mom was emotionally challenging for me. Ever since her Aunt (the mother that raised her passed away), she had become extremely depressed. By this time, she was deeply into drugs. It was very hard to hide it. I caught her a few times smoking her pipe, or she'd be passed out asleep with the pipe nearby. A lot of the time, I would watch her go to and from the crack house. There were times I begged and cried for her to stop. None of the kids in the neighborhood liked me because of this. The name calling and jabs were happening every time I walked out of the house. All I heard every day was, "that's why your mom is a crackhead" or "that's why your mom is old as fuck" or "y'all don't have no money because your mom spent it all on crack bum". We had mice inside of our apartment. However, it wasn't as bad as my dad's apartment. I was always afraid to go to sleep or walk around the home. Most of the time, we didn't have much food either.

She stopped cooking by this time. We were eating peanut butter and syrup sandwiches, boiled eggs, hotdogs, and noodles or processed meat sandwiches. I was always humiliated. We were barely attending church. We stopped doing fun stuff like watching our favorite shows, spending time together or going places. We no longer had a car. We either had to ride the bus, walk or ride our bikes wherever we went. We had down graded to a one-bedroom apartment, so we were sharing rooms. There was very little she could hide from me. The older we got, the higher she wanted to be. The higher she wanted to be, the more aggravated she became.

What was different from her choice of drugs and my dad choice of drugs is he was a happy addict. He used heroin powder. The older that I got, the harder it was for him to hide his secrets. I caught him a few times with a straw, mirror and a card sniffing his powder through his nose. When he got high, he got happy. He would take me to the corner store and buy me snacks, allow me to go outside and play with my friends. He was funny, always joking and laughing. I still hated that he did drugs, smoked cigarettes and drank "crown royal" alcohol every time he got a chance. Sometimes he would drink "5 o'clock gin" or beer to put himself to sleep. Watching him do so much to either sleep or cope, made me never want to do any of it. I hated watching grownups having to depend on substance to get through their days. His friends would come over at the beginning of the month (the first week of each month) to join him getting high and having a drink. It was kind of like my pay week too. They were all pretty much happy. They would basically pay me to get lost. Sometimes my dad would be having so much fun with his friends that he let me stay out past the curfew time. Those were the times I would be outside having a ball with my friends.

Back home with my mom was totally different. Whether she was high or not, I was miserable. She was mad when she wasn't high or sleeping when she was. When she was asleep I wasn't allowed to do anything besides watch tv. By the time she woke up I was in trouble about something I either did or didn't do. The only time I really had a break from being emotionally abused was when my nieces and nephews came over. We used to play sega genesis or Nintendo the most. When we weren't playing video games, we were watching 106 and Park on BET or MTV jams. We used to create our own routines dances like the artists we were watching on tv.

We would also go outside and play, go bike riding throughout the neighborhood when (we weren't supposed to), play on top of our apartment roof (definitely weren't supposed to be doing that), or play cards. When my nieces came over, it was always a good ol time, considering nobody in my neighborhood wanted to play with me.

This was fine with me anyway because most of the kids that were my age were growing up too fast. They were having sex, drinking alcohol, cursing, running away from home, skipping school, smoking weed, fighting, and even driving cars. I wasn't in a rush to grow up. Being an adult looked sad and stressful. Plus, my mom instilled in my head that if you ever have sex, you would expose yourself to HIV, which is what she had. I wasn't entirely sure what that was, but I knew I didn't want it. She said the virus would eventually take her life one day. "A virus can kill you" is what she drilled into my head. I thought to myself often, 'I don't think I ever want to have sex. What was the point?' I thought. After everything my mom has been going through, no boy was important enough for me to, for one, face the consequences of my mom finding out what I've done, and two, lose my life over it. I didn't want to be sick, depressed or turn to drugs to cope everyday like I saw my mom. Either way, neither option was worth the risk. I often was teased by boys and was called a baby, scary, and anything else related to being afraid to have sex. The girls would laugh an d say things like "how long are you going to hold onto your v-card? it's not that big of a deal. It feels good and it would help you gain weight". Back then I was obsessed with having some weight on my body. I was 5'6 and a half weighing barely 100lbs. I hated being small and tall. It seemed as if everyone had done it and was enjoying this good life except for me. For a long time I was fine with that though. I thought to myself "at least I'm not being exposed. I would rather be a toothpick than to be sick".

The older my mom got, the sicker she became. Not only was she no longer attending church, but she also stopped taking her medication altogether. However, she never stopped using drugs. Maybe it was the drugs that told her to give up because that's exactly what she did. She used to say she was tired, and she was ready to die. She said she was waiting for my brother to come home so she could make sure I was okay. She wanted me to live with my brother, I'm assuming because my dad was using drugs as well. They both woke up everyday, almost living in the days with no purpose or having intentional days. It was more like waking up everyday just to get to the next day every single day. If that makes any sense. The older I got, the more aware I became. I told myself "when I grow up, they're not going to have to worry about anything." Having good grades was essential to me. I was taught in order to become successful, having a good education is the only way to get there. I made sure my gpa was no lower than a 3.5 on every report card. This means the C's weren't acceptable for me. My report cards would have only A's and B's.

I had a mission and my goal was to get through school so I can move my parents in with me and they would never have to go to a soup kitchen, have bugs or mice or look at no one else for help. My sisters and older cousins (from my Aunty Carry) weren't helping my mom at all, my mom said. I remember hearing her cry out of frustration and say after all she's done, will do and is doing for so many people, nobody loves her enough to help her. She said, "they see me weak, sick and trying to do better but won't lift a finger to help me when I'm down. Instead they see me and laugh and tell their friends she's just a crackhead like I can't hear them or my ears are broken.".

"Yes I take drugs but I'm human. I love my family but my family dont love me back. The ones that did are all dead. My brothers, sisters, the love of my life, my parents, everyone is just gone." she said. "The system took my son. All I have is you, which I don't know why I had you so late or you would have grown. But the difference between you and my other daughters is I believe that you would look out for me. Your sisters love their men more than me and think that I'm too contagious to come over their homes or even give me a hug." She went on to say that "they wouldn't even allow me in their homes to use their toilet". She ranted the same things all the time and would hold me while crying her eyes out. I felt so helpless. I tried to cheer her up with my words or I made her favorite sandwiches.

I was no angel. I did my fair share of taking advantage of her when she was sick and can't move or when she was high. I would talk back, don't do my chores the way she liked, ride my bike pass where I was allowed, run away to my sisters house if I knew I'll get in trouble. She would send me to the store to purchase her cigarettes, I would sometimes lie and say they were out or I would break them in half or hide them from her. I hated those cigarettes. There were times I would deliberately not do something that she asked when I knew she was too weak to catch me if I ran. I would tell my daddy on her so they can be mad at each other and get into an argument (in hopes) I could go over his house to get away from her. I would hide the things she would whoop me with which always got her angrier. If she couldn't find her belt or Mr. Stick (her back scratcher) she would then start hitting me with anything she saw first. Rather it was a shoe, boot, book, cord, hanger, a can, or even a radio. Whatever was nearest to her is what I got hit with. Sometimes I wouldn't go fill her prescriptions if I was mad at her and I knew she couldn't walk to get it herself. I'm not proud at all for the way I treated her. I wish I could take it all back for causing the stress I put on her. She would put so much pain and responsibilities on me. She made me feel like it was my fault that the things that happened to her happened. I felt like I was being punished for stuff I had no control over. Now that I'm older I see she had no outlet, no therapist and not that many people she could trust. I was the closest to her so it was natural of her to take everything out on me. As she said, I was all that she had. She had a best friend but it was rumored that her and my dad may have done something behind my mom's back. I'm not entirely sure what actually happened. I just remembered my mom saying "Edith isn't your godmother anymore and you're not allowed to ever talk to her again." That was the end of that story.

On December 1, 2001, our apartment was caught on fire. My mom and I fell asleep with candles lit, and one must've fallen on the floor. Our electricity was shut off due to no payments. I was always afraid of the dark because of my experiences with spirits, so I didn't blow out all of the candles. She fell asleep high in the bedroom, and I fell asleep on the couch after her. I assumed that the candles would just blow out on their own. I had no idea leaving them lit would potentially cost us our lives. I remember dreaming about some unfamiliar person screaming "WAKE UP" in my ear very loudly. When I woke up, I noticed smoke and fire everywhere. I was terrified. I ran into my mom's bedroom and woke her up. She woke up in a state of confusion, grabbed me and rushed us out of the front door. We lived on the second floor, but my cousins lived directly underneath us. We ran downstairs to tell them to call 911 and to make sure they were okay. Thank God they were. We lost a lot in that fire. The things we were able to save, we were able to move into my sister's house across town on Jefferson Avenue. Since the fire was our fault, we had to immediately vacate the premises.

Chapter 8
Questions I never received answers for

We ended up moving in with my sister Terri. It seems like when we moved with my oldest sister, my mom became weaker and sicker. There were days she couldn't walk, she couldn't move, and the days she was able to, she could only move with a cane. Her body was breaking down slowly. She started taking her medications again, but by then, I think it was too late to reverse her health condition. Not long after moving in with Terri, my mom had her first stroke. I can't remember if she had the stroke before or after my sister admitted her into a nursing home, but the timing wasn't far from each other. I remember my mother begging Terri not to admit her into a nursing home, saying that's how her mom died. She asked my other sister Ariel if she could stay with her but her boyfriend at the time said no. He said he doesn't want anyone who has HIV around him or his family. Although it was my sister's biological kids (not his), she agreed with him and told her she couldn't live with them. I never understood this. Ariel had her own house, her abusive boyfriend lived with her. How was he able to make that decision? Because Pooh was still in prison, they collectively came up with the decision to admit her into a nursing home. Terri lived with her boyfriend in his home. He randomly decided that he no longer wanted my mom in his basement so he told Terri she had to go. Terri wasn't working full time so maybe she didn't want to take on the responsibility of caring for her sick mom and someone else was already taking care of her financially. I'm not sure of her reasoning behind not fighting more to care for her mom, I just know as soon as she was admitted into the nursing home, she died almost immediately afterwards.

Just a few weeks after being in the nursing home, she had another stroke. She was able to speak, but her words weren't formed in whole sentences. She was almost speaking like a baby. We had to write a lot down to communicate. However, she could understand everything and everyone clearly. She was also only able to use the wheelchair. No more walking with a cane.

She was declining so badly, so fast. I remember my dad took me to go see her a week before my 14th birthday. By this time, she wasn't speaking or walking at all. The nurses and nursing assistants weren't taking very good care of her. She couldn't speak, so they took advantage of this. They weren't doing range of motion, changing her lining and diapers when they were supposed to,. Sometimes they weren't even feeding her. We would ask her certain questions, and she would respond with either a nod, a noise or just cry. But she still understood when we spoke. I remember taking photos of her; she made the loudest noises and cried hard. I knew she didn't want me to take those pictures, but I knew the day was coming when I had to finally say goodbye. I needed something to hold on to, so I snapped the pictures anyway. It hurt her so bad I could tell in her eyes. I explained to her that Pooh wanted some pictures. She kept shaking her head no. I didn't realize from her point of view what I was doing to her. I still have those pictures today. I could never look at them, though. When I left the hospital, I cried as if she had just died that day.

I remember begging God to please give me more time. I would pray on my knees, before i ate, while walking around the house, at school, I would pray every time I thought of my mom. If it was up to me I would've moved into the nursing home with her. My heart felt like it was bleeding outside of my chest. I never felt this kind of abandonment before. I felt so alone like no one in the world could understand me. I didn't understand how to express my true feelings out loud. I just kept them bottled in and cried when no one was watching. I didn't know life without my mom. I mean I knew other people lost their moms but I thought mine was different like Jo can make it through whatever life throws at her. She has been doing it all her life, what makes this time any different is what I was telling myself. I told God, I would do anything I needed to do to keep her alive. Even if I had to die to keep her alive. I said "God my mom told me something about moving mountains and crossing seas, I'll even do that. I'll walk on fire or do whatever you tell me to do. Just please keep her alive. This world needs her more than me". I felt so helpless and scared. I didn't want to feel anymore. No pain, no anger, I didn't even want to be happy. Smiling hurt me.

People tried to cheer me up but how could I laugh when the person I loved more than I loved myself was in the condition that she was in? My whole life revolved around my mom. She was the love of my life, my protector, my provider, my best friend, my therapists, my teacher. She was everything to me. "I needed her. She still needed to teach me stuff. My brother needed her home for when he got out of prison. There was no way all of this could just go away. If she's not here, what does that leave me and Pooh?" I wrote in a letter to God. I needed her to be alive. I needed her to get better. I needed her to get out of that nursing home. I needed her to go on one more bike ride with me. I need her to tell me one more story of her upbringing. I needed her to do my hair again. I needed her to yell at me even though it might hurt. I needed her to hug me and tell me that everything was going to be okay. I needed her to protect me from life. Throughout my eighth-grade year, I moved 3 times. I went from Terri's house to Ariel's house and back to my dad's house. I never changed schools though. I just always caught different buses. I was finishing up my last year in middle school. I was promoted (out of sympathy from my 5th grade teachers) to middle school without participating in my elementary school graduation. This would be my first time participating in a graduation event at school. With all this going on, I had to finish 8th grade with good grades and test scores. I figured she would be alive long enough for me to get a successful job so I can get her out of that nursing home.

God gave me more time with her like I prayed for... But not for long. Mom had a third stroke on May 28th, 2002. The third stroke was too aggressive for her to survive through. Her HIV virus had already turned into full blown aids. Her immune system was extremely weak. It was a miracle that she survived as long as she did. All I kept hearing in my head was "I'm tired.

I'm ready to be with the people who loved me" was the words she used to say to me. Immediately I felt raged. I thought to myself "you are one selfish ass person! Why would you stop taking your medication? Did I not mean anything at all to you at all? My love wasn't good enough because I'm a child? Why wasn't I enough?" How could you possibly think that you could take a break from medications that you were instructed to take everyday then change your mind and think that everything was going to be alright? I thought you were smarter than that!".

My mind was racing. I was mad at everyone. I hated her, God, my sisters, my dad, my brother, everyone!

As I was walking from the bus stop coming from school, excited that I made the dean's list. I couldn't wait to tell everyone that not only was I graduating, but I was graduating with honors. I found one piece of happiness this day and couldn't wait to share the good news. As I walked to Ariel's house, her oldest daughter (my niece) was on the porch crying, waiting for me to return from school. She broke down in tears when she saw me approaching the stairs to the house. I knew why she was crying, but I pretended not to know. A part of me thought there was no way she was crying over what I thought she was crying over, so maybe she was crying because her mom and her mom's boyfriend got into a heated argument again. He was extremely abusive so it wouldn't be a shock. By the time I reached the porch, she said a word to me that made me feel like my ears had fallen off. My body shut completely down. I fell down right where I stood. It was like my body ran out of gas. My thoughts were racing so fast. Once I got enough energy to snap back into reality, I asked, "What did you just say to me?" She said it again, "Grandma died!" I ran into the house and ran upstairs to find Ariel to confirm this news. As I was running up the stairs, I heard the whole house crying and sobbing. I no longer wanted to see Ariel so I ran into the restroom and locked myself in there instead. I couldn't handle it. I didn't want to be bothered. I didn't want to be touched. I didn't want to be looked at. I didn't want to speak to anyone. I locked myself inside the bathroom for hours. Whoever needed to use the restroom had to wait. I wasn't opening that door for anyone unless they were coming to tell me it was all a joke.

Eventually, when I walked out of the restroom it was night time. Later, I walked into the room I was sleeping in with my nieces and continued to cry until I made myself sick. I felt like I had died. I felt something leave my body the more I screamed. To this day, I'm not sure that whatever left my body that day ever had came back. I was so numb. Almost to the point that my emotions were burned out. I felt so much anger for everyone. I blamed everyone, especially God. I was so confused. How I'd live now is what I kept thinking to myself. There's no such thing as life continuing, right? I mean how? What do I do now? Where do I go? What does living mean now? How am I supposed to eat? How was I supposed to breathe? How was I supposed to speak? I never wanted to smile again, there was no point. I never wanted to talk to anybody about it. It wasn't like they could bring her back. I didn't want to watch tv because all I saw was her favorite shows. I didn't want to go outside because I kept seeing her face. I didn't want to listen to any other music than Yolanda Adams because only her music helped me hear her voice. I only wanted to hear her voice so she could answer all of my questions. I didn't want to go to sleep because I was afraid she would come to my dreams and leave me more heart broken. I just didn't want anything life had to offer if it wasn't bringing her back.

Chapter 9
The transition

I remember at the funeral I thought I saw her moving and breathing. I was really hallucinating. I was even trying to get everyone to say they saw it too. Something in me kept saying just go wake her up so she can show everybody she was just playing. But the pastor started talking and ended up shutting the casket. At this time, I knew it wasn't a joke. This was real life. Right before the funeral Terri came over to Ariel's house just to tell us that she wasn't going to the funeral. She said she can't go to another funeral. So she started to dance and sing and say "we're celebrating her life not her death, so cheer up!". I wanted to call her while at the funeral and curse her out to tell her there was no celebration going on. She's gone and you're not here! I continued to look around because I just knew she was going to show up. There's no way she's not coming to her own mother's funeral. Terri and I were a lot closer than Ariel and I were. I needed Terri by my side to tell me it was going to be okay. I waited, I looked around, there was even a seat saved for her. But she never showed. My brother was able to attend the first part of the funeral in shackles. I haven't seen him since I was a little kid in person. We Kept contact through phone calls and mail. At first, I was scared. He looked very different from when I was a child. However, that fear went away fast. I remember thinking I loved my brother so much and he was standing in front of me, in flesh. The prison guards wouldn't allow us to touch or talk for long. "Why can't he just get out right now?" I thought. But then I thought that when he comes home, I'm going to have to live with him. At that moment, that's not what I wanted.

After the funeral, I moved in with my dad after begging and pleading my case. Everyone kept saying that it was best to finish the school year at Ariel's house. In my mind, nobody knew what was best for me except me. They said "your dad is sick and old, staying with Ariel is best." I said "I know what's best for me. If he's sick and old, that is all the more reason why I need to be there for him. I couldn't save my mom, but I'm forsure going to save my dad! I don't care how many buses I'll have to take to get to school, I will finish it with my dad". Everyone agreed with me so I moved back with him. My dad could never tell me no. After moving from Ariel's house, I wanted some of my mom's belongings. To my surprise, Terri's boyfriend threw all of our stuff out without notifying us (well, me anyway). All of my mom's memories were gone. Everything that was important to me was just gone like a swift transition. I hated him for this. I hated my sister for allowing this to happen. The anger I felt was so deep that if I had the opportunity, I would have blown his house while he was sleeping inside. My mom taught me that no matter what happens in life, to never let someone have so much control over you that you hate them. She always told me that God doesn't support hate, but I hated him. I can't honestly say that feeling has ever changed. I used the word hate a lot back then but I didn't truly hate anyone besides my sister's boyfriends. I asked God to forgive my heart but don't take away the way I felt about them. I enjoyed the feeling because I knew when I got older that I would get my lick back with the both of them.

Moving back with my dad was different this time. I poured all of my emotions onto my father. I wasn't going to visit my mom's house to visit on the weekends anymore. I couldn't call her to tell her how my days went. I cried myself to sleep all night and woke up to cry some more every day. Some days I was okay. Other days I wasn't. Then there were days I was just numb. I felt empty and lost inside. A part of me felt like that I wanted to continue living for her. I wanted to do everything just like her or how she would've done it. I was stuck between trying to take on her old problems and making them my own or making her proud. I wanted to feel something from her. Even if it was feeling her pain. But I knew how much my education meant to her. I was a couple of weeks from finishing the 8th grade, so I had to attend school. I didn't want to at all. I couldn't focus. It took everything I had inside to get out of bed everyday. While I was physically there, my mental state was completely gone. I literally just showed up every day and did no work. One day, I was sent to the principal's office for a mental check. She was asking me all of these questions, but I had no answers. She just stood up from her seat, walked towards me, and hugged me tightly. I couldn't stop the tears from dripping down my face.

    Thinking about the day of graduation gave me some sort of satisfaction when it was time to prepare for the ceremony.. I knew she would be very proud of me, so I had to find a reason to keep going so that I could walk across that stage. The ceremony was expected to be held at Finny High School. I asked my older cousin Ronna if I could wear my real hair straight down my back. My mom didn't like my hair straightening much, but I felt this was a special occasion. My mom only liked my hair in a ponytail or braids. Ronna did my hair as I asked, and I fell in love. My hair was dark brown and came to the middle of my back. My natural hair is curly and wavy so it looks shorter until straightened. I went home to my dad to show him my hair and asked what he was wearing to the graduation. He told me he wasn't planning on coming. This broke my heart. I couldn't understand why he would say that to me. In my mind, there were no options. He was the last living parent that I had left. I don't even remember him giving me an explanation of why he wasn't coming. I went to my room and dived in my pillows to cry. He came inside my room, and I unleashed everything I felt inside onto him. I told him he's not allowed to die. He can't leave me. I said I needed him. I said I needed him to get off of the drugs. I wasn't completely sure what was going on with his health, but I knew something was going on. He wasn't himself. I begged him to come to the graduation. He still said he wasn't going but he'll be home when I return. He grabbed me and held me tight. I told him I was afraid my mom would visit me in my dreams, and I was too afraid to talk to her. I didn't completely understand that I'd never see her again. Although I've experienced some death prior to my mom's death, this one was quite different. The pain and confusion were too much to handle. He looked at me and said, "I will always be here for you. Even if I'm not here, I'm here." At first that didn't make me feel better at all. I asked, "What do you mean if you're not here? Where are you going?" He replied, "Nowhere, I'm just letting you know that I'll never leave you!"

On the day of graduation, Ronna came to support me. That was it. No one else showed up for me. No siblings, aunts, cousins, parents, nobody. I tried not to get into my feelings about it because all of my friends were trying to cheer me up. The ceremony was beautiful until all the students on the principals and dean's lists received a special shout-out. When it was my turn, the principal let everyone know that my mom had passed away just two weeks prior. I felt so embarrassed and ashamed. In my mind, I ran off the stage and went home. But in reality, I was standing there crying. She grabbed me and told me all these encouraging words, but I needed my father present at that moment. I needed him to be in the front row. But he wasn't. I felt so abandoned and cheated. Everyone else's parents were in attendance. Although I was grateful for my cousin's support, I wanted my father to be present as well. After all, in my mind, I did it for them (him and my mother). I wanted my parents to be proud of me. I came from barely passing to a promoted grade to the dean's list and was on the honor roll my entire 8th grade. My father always told me school and education were so important, and when he and my mom were growing up, they didn't have the opportunities I had. Yet, he wasn't there to see what I'd done.

When I received my plaque, I whispered, looked up, and said, "This is the first of many. I will keep making you proud."

When choosing a high school, my dad wanted me to attend a school the neighborhood kids weren't going to. I hated it when my parents did this. Everyone was going to Kettering High, but my dad decided to enroll me in Southeastern. I asked if I could go to King or Cass Tech, but he said those schools were too far and it would take too many buses to get there. Not to mention I was supposed to put those applications in to apply for those schools months ago. So Southeastern I went. High school wasn't that bad. It was a lot different than middle school. There was so much peer pressure everywhere. If you weren't driving a car, having sex, or skipping school, you were considered a lame (also known as a square or unpopular). My dad taught me not to follow the crowd, so I wasn't easily moved to do what everyone else was doing. In order for me not to be a part of the "lame" crew, I had to at least come to school looking good. My dad and I received monthly checks. Because he was injured in the military and Chrysler. They both had to pay him a disability check. I was receiving checks from the day I was born because I was his descendant. My mom never gave me the financial freedom to do what I wanted with my checks, but my dad did. Every 3rd of the month, he gave me $500 and taught me how to budget. I would put some money aside to buy my lunch daily (chicken wings, hot Cheetos, and clear fruit at the cafeteria), hair money, bus money to get back and forth to school and finally, shopping money.

In high school, I had to turn it up a notch. I went from being bullied to being popular. I tried out for the cheer team but didn't make varsity because I couldn't flip. I was good at everything else but those flips had me paralyzed. I didn't want to be on the jr. varsity, so I went to the pom-pom squad. They were cooler than JV cheerleaders. We still attended the games to hype the crowds up. The girls on the squad started to become too grown for me. They had grown men as boyfriends. The grown men would attend the games for them, sitting in the stands to cheer them on. It made me comfortable so I didn't hang out with them. After only a few games I quit the squad and joined the tennis team. I was only there for a short period of time too. I think that only lasted about two weeks. I quit because they worked out too much. I didn't like working out at all. Lastly, I joined the step team. I loved the step team. It reminded me of the movie, "Stomp the Yard". Joining that team was when I first started thinking about colleges and sororities. The girls on the team were like-minded. I fit right in with these girls. It was then I started to feel something inside of me. Finally, I was able to smile and laugh again. I was able to look forward to something everyday. The girls on the team were very kind and supportive. When someone was struggling to learn the material or routine, the other girls would go above and beyond to assist with whatever is needed to get each other on the right track.

I had to start over in the friend category because almost everyone attending my previous middle school ended up attending Finny High. The neighborhood kids were attending Kettering High, so I basically had to start from scratch with the friends. The friends I started to make were cool. The closer I got to them, the more of an influence they had on me. With my friends and nieces all peer pressuring me, I started thinking about having sex more. I wanted to see what the hype was all about. I had a sex education class at this time, so I was learning that everything my mom taught me wasn't the complete truth. They taught us the importance of using condoms, birth control and abstinence. They also taught us about pregnancies, STDs and so much more. They even had us bring baby dolls home for weeks to give us parenting experience. It was then I told myself that I'd never have kids. That doll got on my last nerves. The teachers said that each doll had cameras inside of the eyes to watch how we cared for them for a grade. I had to figure out why it cried, and it constantly cried at random times. I had to feed it, change the diaper and talk to it while rocking it to make the crying stop. I even had to find a sitter to look after it if I wanted to go outside to hang out with my friends. I said if I had to deal with a real child like this, do not sign me up.

Yet, I still wanted to have sex just to see what everyone was talking about, and since my mom wasn't around to beat me up, "why not?" I thought.

The kids in our neighborhood were all very close. We all grew up together. I've known most of them since kindergarten. A lot of the boys from school and from my neighborhood liked me. But it was only one I'd let my guard down to cross that line with. Deon was a year and a half younger than I was, but I was in love with him. He was tall, cute, and athletic and his smile was everything to me. He always kept a girlfriend. I always kept a boyfriend in our separate schools. I used to spend the night at his house because his sister and I were close. She was also younger than me, but we got along really well. I loved his mom dearly. She always cooked big homemade meals and made room for me at their dinner table so I wouldn't have to go to my Aunt's house or that soup kitchen. She'll even let me bathe over when our hot water wasn't on. One night, he and I stayed up really late, talking and playing games like we usually do. I asked him if he was a virgin, and he replied, "No, at our age, who's even a virgin anymore?" I said, "You are younger than me, how are you not a virgin? Who let you hit?" He then laughed and said his ex-girlfriend. Then he asked me if I was still one. I hesitated and responded, "Yes, but I want you to be my first." as I watched for his body language to respond to my words, I instantly regretted what I had just said. He asked when I wanted to do this? I responded, "Not tonight, but I'll let you know whenever I am ready." He was so excited. He started being extra nice to me from that night forward.

I had Deon waiting around until I was ready. He was wrapped around my finger. He started walking me to my apartment when the streetlights came on (he never used to do that). He started buying me snacks at the corner store. He even let me play street sports with him and his friends. We had a love/dislike relationship. We always argue and then quickly make up. He was like my best friend. We often talked about anything under the sun; then we'd argue or even fight, then be right back laughing. Everyone in the neighborhood thought we were crazy. We shared a bond that was unexplainable. We still share that even to this day. We can not speak for years and reconnect like we never left. We finally ended up doing it one night while I spent a night in his house. We waited until everyone was asleep to sneak into one of the kids rooms. We started out playing and talking like we always did, but then we kissed. When we kissed, our body temperature aroused. I was so nervous. "This was the moment that was going to change my life" I thought. Oddly, I was wondering if my mom was watching me. I was hoping she wasn't is all I kept secretly whispering to myself. "I can't back out now; I came too far," is all I kept thinking. But the guilt and shame was driving me crazy. As he took my clothes off and put a condom on, he asked me if I was ready. I said we probably needed a towel because everyone said I'd bleed afterwards. He went and grabbed a towel and laid me on top of it. He slid inside me, pumped about 4 times, and said he was done. He was breathing heavily and moved from on top of me. He asked if I was okay then turned over and went to sleep immediately after I assured him that I was fine. As I watched him sleep for a few moments I remembered being so confused. I thought to myself, "Was that it? Is that what all the hype is about? I barely felt anything. I wasn't even bleeding." Those few seconds were uncomfortable, but they were manageable. Nonetheless, I did it. I was a new woman. So I went to wash myself up and went to bed in the girls room where his sister's was located.

Chapter 10

Sex, lies and drugs

When I got back to school the next day, I walked around with my head held high because I was grown (so I thought). I couldn't wait to get home the next day to tell my nieces that I crossed over to the other side. My whole attitude towards everybody had changed. When I started telling people, they laughed and were a bit confused. They said that their experience was bloody, it was painful, it lasted at least 10 minutes and they performed oral sex on each other. They said after the pain, the pleasure came and it was one of the best feelings that they've ever had. My first thought was "don't tell me I have to do that again ". I was so disappointed. I wanted to feel good and have the best feeling experience too but I didn't want to do it again. I felt like I was cheated.

Over time my boyfriend, Noel, and I had grown closer. It has been months since my virginity was taken. Because of my first experience I didn't tell Noel what happened. I had him thinking that I was still a virgin. At first, I didn't want him to be my first because we had only been together a few months. He had a bad boy reputation, always into something. He was also a sweetheart. He was a great listener, catering, protective and thoughtful. However, he lived a fast life, I later found out. He used to go to Southeastern, but I stopped seeing him around the school all of a sudden. He told me he was suspended, but he never returned. For months, I went to his house when I was allowed. We never did anything sexual besides kiss. Even when we were chilling in the room with the door shut. Honestly, I don't know why. He tried to take it to the next level but I was too nervous. I liked how nice he was to me and how he treated me. He treated me like I was all that mattered. His mom was always nice to me as well. Looking back at it now, his mom was a little too nice. She allowed us to stay in his room with the door closed all the time. She would always knock before coming in, saying she didn't want to interrupt his privacy. He never pressured me to do anything. It often crossed my mind how the experience would be if I had sex with him. After a while and many visits later, we did it.

This time was a lot different. After he put the condom on he then slid inside me. It hurted so bad I could barely take it. After so many strokes of him going back and forth I kept trying to feel the pleasure part. He seemed as if was having himself a nice time. He didn't care that his mom was awake and walking around. I never spent the night at Noel's house. I always had to be home before the streetlights came on. He lived about 8 streets away from where I lived. Having sex when everyone was asleep and doing it while everyone was wide awake in the middle of the day was completely different. From the looks of how comfortable he was, I could tell he had done this before. He even told me to turn around so he could switch positions. I'm not sure if we finished, but I begged him to stop. I couldn't take the pain from the second position. Once he stopped, I noticed I was bleeding everywhere. He felt so bad; he thought he did something wrong to me. I just asked if he could walk me home after we were done. He walked me home, apologizing the entire way. I didn't know what to say. I could only think "was he my real first? Everything everyone had told me happened with him. Not Deon, so did the first time count?" I couldn't ask him about it because I already lied to him. In his mind, I was already a virgin. I couldn't talk to Deon about it because I didn't want to look like a hoe in his eyes. Although he already knew I had a boyfriend, he also knew I wasn't having sex with him. I had just slept with him a few months prior. I definitely couldn't talk to my dad about it. I wanted male advice about it for some reason. I figured the females wouldn't know.

He never returned back to school, but every time I saw him, he had so much money. There was no doubt in my mind that he dropped out of school to hustle. He was never the flashy type of hustler. The hustlers I knew were loud, disrespectful, flashy and had a lot of girls trying to get with them. Noel was not like any of that. He was quiet, lowkey, and very humbled. I used to ask him where he was getting so much money to help his mom? He told me he was working. I'm not sure why I never thought to ask more questions. Rumor around school was that he was into selling drugs and may have been gang affiliated. That immediately turned me off. I stopped talking to him immediately. We always shared so much with each other of our life stories together., He knew how I felt about drug dealers. With my parents using drugs, I would never want to talk to anyone in that industry. Of course he denied the allegations and rumors. I didn't believe him though. He tried reaching out to me for a while, but I never returned his calls. Deep down, I knew I should have at least talked to him about it before letting him go completely. My pride wouldn't let me. I never spoke to him again. All of my friends called me stupid for not wanting a drug dealer as a boyfriend. They said he would spoil me and I would have anything I want. I think he even bought himself a car. However, that wasn't the life for me, so I moved on. I thought of him a lot. I had a really deep connection to him. I wanted to talk to my dad about all of this, but I was too afraid of his disappointment more than him being angry at me for what I've done. I was very open with my dad about almost everything. Telling him I had sex wasn't one of those times, let alone two different boys. At this time, I had to just keep quiet and never do it again was the solution I gave myself.

Going into my sophomore year of high school, life was starting to have some color again. My dad and I have grown closer than we've ever had. My brother was released from prison after being locked up for 14 years. My social life was better. No more being teased for being tall, dark, slim, making fun of my clothes, hair, or being called ugly and stupid. When my brother came home, I was so excited but also nervous. I haven't seen him since momma's funeral. The man I've always known was only a voice or hand written letters. We had to get to know each other outside of the brief conversations. When he came home, he decided to reside in Lansing, MI with his then girlfriend. He came to pick me up to spend some time with him for a week during the summer. While I was visiting, he was talking to me about his plans to have me move in with him. I didn't like that idea at all. My social life was really great at the time. I loved my school and my friends. Not to mention, ever since my mom died, I was super clingy to my father.

I really didn't like being away from him. I didn't tell my concerns of discomfort to Pooh. I just started disliking him for even thinking of taking me away from my father. Yes, we were poor, and my dad was old, but I loved my life there. Pooh was thinking because he promised momma when he came home that he would finish raising me. He thought that it was his responsibility to give me the good life my mom told him to give me. I have never put real thought into going to college until visiting Pooh. He had us riding pass colleges and talking about submitting college applications. Up onto that point college was more like a fantasy than a reality. I never thought of having my own car until Pooh put it in my head that he would buy me one if I keep up my grades. He was even going to buy a house so that I could have my own room at his house. While I appreciated his good intentions, I didn't want that at the time. I didn't know how to express that to him. The girlfriend he had at the time made my decision much easier to not live with them. I didn't like her at all. She was mean, rude and a liar. As a result of this, I made it clear that I wanted to stay home with my dad, and so I did.

Shortly after visiting pooh, he was arrested and taken back to jail for violation of his probation. He was sentenced to 2 years. As winter quickly approached, my dad suddenly started getting sick. He went back and forth to the hospital, but he kept it a secret from me as to what the reasons behind it were. He was in and out of the hospital so much he even got me a new Motorola cell phone. For so long, he did not believe in having a cell phone. He said he didn't trust them. Cell Phones and computers began to grow in popularity but that was too new for my dad to support. This was a big deal back in 2003. Your family had to have some money for a kid to have a cell phone and minutes. Back then we had to purchase minutes to talk or text. My dad always said, "We don't need cell phones when we have a house phone." But because he wasn't home so much, he said I needed a phone so he could reach me. He was in and out of the hospital for a couple of months. While he was away, I would stay at Deon's mom's house so I could get a ride to school from his grandad who lived across the street.

Chapter 11
It was all a dream

On January 4, 2004, we had a really big snowstorm in Detroit. Students were getting ready to get off the Christmas/New Year holiday break to return to school. My dad asked if I wanted to spend the night at Deon's house even though he wasn't in the hospital. He said the snow would be really deep in the morning because it was expected to snow overnight. There were rare occasions when they shut our schools down due to weather conditions back then. This took me by surprise because I would usually have to beg him to spend the night over at a friend's house if he wasn't in the hospital no matter what the weather was. He was just released from the hospital just a couple of weeks ago for upper respiratory complications. His coughing and wheezing were getting worse. I asked him the whole weekend if he could please go admit himself back into the hospital. He would brush it off every time I brought it up. But this particular Sunday night, I sat him down and cried my heart out, begging him to go back to the hospital. I reminded him of how important he was to me and that I couldn't bear losing another parent. I just wouldn't be able to handle it, I told him. I continued to say that "without Pooh, I had no one else." At the time, I strongly disliked my sisters for how they treated my mom before she died. I had no interest in having a relationship with them at all. I tolerated them to be able to keep a relationship with my nieces and nephews. After telling him all of this, he agreed to see a doctor the next morning while I was in school.

He then stood up and gave me my new cell phone and told me not to give his sister my new number. He also said not to answer if she calls the house phone when I come home from school. This came as a shock to me because he never said anything like this before. He and his sister were extremely close. He also said that I shouldn't answer or speak to our cousin "Spring". To my knowledge, they were best friends, almost like brothers. I didn't know what was happening, but I learned a long time ago to stay out of the grown-up business. I always regretted not asking him "why?". So, I asked 'how are you going to get to the hospital?'. He said his friend "Moore" was coming to pick him up first thing in the morning to take him. "Don't worry, everything will be fine." He continued, "I will call you when you get out of school tomorrow.

They probably will admit me." he said. I packed my bag to go to spend the night at my friend's Shalonda's house (aka Deon house) so that I could get a ride the next day with their grandfather. He returned to the room, gave me $500 cash and hugged me really tight. He held me differently this time. He hugged me a little longer than usual. He walked me out the door to walk me to my friend's house.

That night, I fell asleep praying. I can't remember the exact words I said, but I remember talking to God that night. I felt something, but I didn't know what the feeling meant. After dinner and a bath, I fell asleep. That night, I dreamed that my dad was in this white environment. I couldn't tell if it was a white room, white outside, or white cloud. I just knew it was pure white. He sat me down calmly and began to speak to me. I don't remember the complete details of what he was saying, but I do remember him saying, "Do me a favor?" he asked. "What's that?"I said. He said "I love you. But you can't come with me so dont chase me". I remember being a bit confused saying, "I don't understand what that means." He said, "I'm going to go away, but promise me not to chase me!" I was still confused and asked, "What do you mean?" He said, "You cannot follow me. Do not try to run after me. That's not how it goes." I remember falling to my knees in tears. I said "I feel so hurt. Why does my heart feel so heavy? What is wrong? Make the pain stop. Where are you going?" He said some more stuff but I can't remember everything. I just remember him talking to me and me feeling so sad.. I sat there and waited for him to come back after he walked off. As I was waiting for him to return, I started hearing Shalondas mom screaming my name. "Everybody, get up! Time for school! Get up right now!" She demanded. I jumped up frantically, thinking I was late. I hurried, got dressed and got in the car to go to school.

It felt like a regular day to return to school. Because it was the first day of school from our break, everybody was dressed in their best outfits. This is the time where you showed off your christmas gifts gear. Students would go back and forth to the pencil sharpener so everyone could see their new shoes as they walked all the way to the front of class. Or they would pretend that they have to go to the bathroom so everyone can see their new outfit when they walk out of the classroom door. During my second period, I heard my name being called to the office from the announcement system. "Julena Coleman, report to the main office." It felt like bricks fell into my stomach. As I walked to the office, I saw my cousins standing there waiting for me. Ronna and her mom were there holding and consoling each other.. When I saw them, I instantly knew I was about to receive the worst news that would change my life forever. I felt like my niece was standing on the front porch waiting for me to arrive all over again. The feeling felt so familiar. I started crying as soon as I made eye contact.

I quickly walked inside of the office and watched my cousin's lips as she said, "I'm so sorry, Lena…your dad was found dead!". I'm not entirely sure if she said anything after that. My ears instantly started ringing. I went def. I thought I was shot in the stomach. I thought I died. My ears felt like they were bleeding. My heart felt like she snatched it out of my chest. I felt like my lungs collapsed because I couldn't catch my breath. I wanted to take my eyes out of the sockets from seeing anything else she was trying to tell me. I blacked out. I'm not sure how I got in the car. I just remember riding to my Aunt's house from school. I tried to jump out of the car many times while Ronna was driving to run to our apartments to see for myself. I didn't believe them. I didn't trust them. "My dad just warned me last night not to talk to them," was all I kept thinking. Of course, they kept restraining me until we pulled up to their house. I remember being so angry and agitated. Upon arriving at my Aunt's house, I went straight to the bathroom to scream from the bottom of my lungs and cry. When I walked out of the bathroom, there were suits laid out on the kitchen table. I asked, "Who are these for?" Ruth walked in and said, "Which one do you like most for him?" I went into a state of shock. "I just discovered this news not even 20 minutes ago about his passing. I'm thinking "I had just seen my dad, touched him, talked to him, heard his voice less than 10 hours ago, and you're asking which suit I like most to bury him in?". I wanted to choke her right where she stood. At this point, I was on fire. I tried every trick I could think of to try to sneak out of the house and run to the apartments. But I was never able to escape.

Ruth had me stay with them until a couple of days before the funeral day. I never slept through a complete night again. I was too afraid to fall asleep. Every time I woke up, I was faced with the reality that I was all alone. Both of my Parents were gone. For some strange reason, I wanted to miss my Grandparents that I never met. I never had that feeling before. I wanted to touch and hold people I would never be able to. I felt abandoned. I felt like I wanted to die. There was a big part of me telling myself it's completely impossible to just never see them again. That's just not possible. That's not how life works. When I do see them I'm going to be so mad at them for this. I think I was going crazy. My thoughts were running a thousand times an hour and three times more at night. I did not feel comfortable there. I felt like there were evil spirits all through that house. So I asked if I could stay with Shalonda for a while. At first they gave me a hard time but I started acting up. I started being disrespectful so they ended up agreeing that I could go. Ruth told me that I was forbidden to visit the apartment. She said it was too traumatizing and I shouldn't be there. She told me to write down where all of my stuff was located. She said they would pack my things for me. This made my blood boil.She only packed about two garbage bags worth of my stuff. I never received all of my belongings and nothing of his to remember him by. She had the landlord change the lock and instructed him not to let me in if I asked.

I was told that his cause of death was lung cancer. To my knowledge, he never had lung cancer or any other form of cancer. They said our cousin "Spring" went into the apartment that morning to take him to the hospital. When he arrived, supposedly my dad was lying half up on the couch with a cigarette in his hand, hunched over, unresponsive. This story was always suspicious to me. It just never made complete sense. It had me questioning everything. I couldn't think straight. Two days before the funeral, I couldn't take it anymore. I asked if I could move in with Shalonda and her family permanently. She agreed that I could stay there only for a few nights, but after the funeral, I would have to come back there. I also wasn't allowed to attend school.

Chapter 12
Money, Power, No Respect

January 14th, 2004, would be the next time that I saw my Father. This time, it was in a casket. I wasn't allowed to ride in the family's car because I stayed with Shalonda. I arrived with them like they were my family. In my head, they were. I kept thinking during the funeral, "Something isn't right. This doesn't feel right." During the funeral, the army reserves did a presentation and gave Ruth a military flag. I didn't know what it meant, so I thought nothing of it. After the funeral, a few people approached me telling me that I was his closest kin. I was supposed to get his honorable United States flag. I went to the director of the funeral home and asked how'd this happened. He said, "Let me go check my records; give me one second." He came back and said, "We have documentation stating that he leaves no dependents behind." with his sister's signature. I thought I was watching a movie. I just couldn't believe what I was hearing. I walked up to my Aunt to ask her what was going on. Why didn't I receive his flag and why did she sign that he didn't have children? She said you will get it when you find a stable home. I don't want you to lose it. She said we would talk about it at the repass and said it was inappropriate to talk about that right there. She said to meet the family at the repass in about an hour. I asked "what about the cemetery?". I have been to enough funerals to know that after funerals, we are supposed to go to the grave site. She said that only the people who were riding in the family car will go straight there, and everyone else will receive the address. I agreed and walked off not thinking much of it.

She never sent the address. I called and went to her house, but no one was there. So, I went back to my Shalonda's house to wait until I received a call for instructions. I never received a call. I waited the whole day. Shalonda's mom didn't have a car so I couldn't ride past the house as much as I wanted to. The next day, I was able to get a ride to my Ruth's house to ask her what happened. She stated she thought she gave me the address to everything. That was straight bullshit and she knew it. She said "you would've been there if you rode in the family car. You wouldn't have missed anything!" I wanted nothing more but to get out of this lady's house. She said "and you can't go back there.". She told me I was still a minor and forbidden to see them again. I said, "I want to live with my sisters, then." In my mind, anywhere was better than being there. So, I moved to Dexter and Davison on Detroit's west side with my sister, Ariel.

Moving in with Ariel meant I had to switch schools and start my life all over in the middle of the school year. The next day I moved in with Ariel. The very first thing she did was take me to the Social Security office to inquire about my benefits. It was at that moment that I knew I may have made a mistake. Ariel instantly viewed me as a financial opportunity gain. Before even enrolling me in school or checking on my well-being or even getting me set up in the house, I was at the social security's office trying to get my checks transferred into her name. It wasn't the best feeling knowing that she only cared about my money, but it was still better than living with my paternal side of the family. When we arrived at the office, we were told that all of my benefits were already switched over to my father's sister's name. This all caught me by surprise because we had just finished his funeral in not less than 24 hours. He passed away a little over a week ago and my benefits have already been switched over multiple times. After the social security office visit, we went to enroll me into a school. I chose to attend Murray-Wright High School, also known as the home of the pilots. This meant taking two buses to school, but I was told they had the best reputation for academics and student behavior out of all the other nearby schools.

Going to Murray-Wright wasn't hard at all. It didn't take me long to make new friends. I actually felt more socially accepted there than I did in Southeastern. This could be because I stopped giving a fuck. After losing my parents back-to-back, it was too hard to care about life and whatever it had to offer. It was days I was freaking out. I would see my parents' faces everywhere. People on the bus looked like them. People at Wendy's looked like them. People walking down the street had faces. Sometimes I would talk to these strangers softly under my breath as if they were my parents. Other times, I would curse God out for making me believe they were still alive. As if God was playing tricks on me. I cried every single day. I was angry, disrespectful and very bitter. I didn't care about almost anything. I used to pray to die. The thoughts of suicide ran through my mind quite often. The only reason I didn't go through with any suicidal plans was because my mom taught me at an early age that any person who takes their own life might not be able to get into heaven. She said that taking the gift of your own life is the only sin that isn't forgiven by God. When I was in those depressed moments, I would tell myself, "If you ever want to see them again, you can't go through with it," so I didn't. But that didn't make me want to care about life.

In school, I would show up but never to classes. I would skip in the halls, play cards, watch the dice game, sneak to the nearby store for food and snacks. Hanging out and socializing with my friends was all I cared about. I had two garbage bags full of my stuff from my dad's house, but it wasn't all of my good stuff. In order to hang around with the cool kids, you have to be one. You had to wear the latest designers clothing and have the latest cellphone. Your hair had to be groomed and you had to have some money. When the third of the month of February came around, I asked Ariel if I could have my money to go shopping and get my hair and nails done. She told me that money had to go towards her bills. She could only give me the bus fare to make it back and forth to school every day for the month. I said, "Well, what about my lunches?" I didn't eat school lunches. I liked the purchased chicken wings or pizza, clear fruit juice and going to the snack store. She told me no, but she would give me more next month. March 3rd came around, and she pulled the same thing but she purchased herself a minivan. Although she had this van, I still had to ride the bus every day. However, she made sure she drove her children to and from school every morning. She said that my school was too far to drive to every day. At that moment, I knew it was time to go. I ended up calling my other sister, Terri. Just like that, back to the east, I went.

Terri lived near Osborn High School on Detroit's east side. Her two girls were already attending

Osborn high, so she wanted me to switch schools. I wasn't having that. I would rather catch 3 buses to school every day than switch schools again. So that's what I did. I caught buses every day to go to school. Not to attend classes but to hang out with my friends. My sister worked at a shopping store called "7 days" on Warren and Conner (on the east side of the city). She always brought clothes home for us. We were all three different sizes so we couldn't share any clothes with one another. She gave me about $300 of my check to do whatever I wanted with it. That was better than what Ariel had done for me when I stayed with her. Sometimes she even made ways for me to get to school from her boyfriend she had at the time.

"Now, I'm living a life," is what I was thinking. We ate whatever we wanted to eat most nights. Terri's rules for her house were more relaxed than Ariel's rules. I didn't have to share my personal space with 5 other kids. Terri had 3 kids, but only 2 lived with her. Her youngest child lived with her father. Terri was almost never home because she was either working or was with her boyfriend. Sometimes, she left her car keys and said not to drive her car unless it was an emergency. None of us had a drivers license or a driving permit but we knew how to drive because my mom taught us when we were in elementary school. Every time she left, it was an emergency for me and my nieces. We enjoyed many joy rides all over town. We would've had company over often if we hadn't had so many roaches. Those roaches were so embarrassing. It seems like they came out of hibernation every time we had company. I never invited anyone over but my nieces did. We would all be watching music videos, playing games, eating takeout and chilling. Life was full of freedom at home and in school. My nieces and I were always close, so living together felt more like sisters than anything else. We all knew each other's business secrets. The same for Ariel's kids. They were just slightly younger than Terri's girls.

Chapter 13

Be careful who you call a friend

One day in school, I was hanging out with my usual crew. We were all skipping classes and hanging out in the hallways like we usually do. One of them, named Carl, said, "I'm about to go home; it's boring here today." I said, "You are about to go all the way home? You are not going to get in trouble for skipping?" He laughed and said, "No, my sister is picking me up. Do you want a ride?" I said, "No, I'm good, my sister is probably home.". He went on to say, "You can stay with me at my sister's house until school lets out, so you won't have to catch the bus home. There's only 2 hours left in the day. You might as well come with us, unless you have some important classes you can't miss?" "Besides, my sister will be there with us and she can take you home when school actually lets out," he went on to say. I agreed to go. After all, he was one of my first friends in Murray. He never gave me any reason to believe that he was physically attracted to me in any way. He said his sister lived a street away from Osborn high. I lived about 7 streets away so it was walking distance away from that location. Getting rides to and from school was always better than catching 2-3 buses a day so why not. When we got to his sister's house, she turned the TV on in the living room for us to watch a movie. She offered us snacks while we chilled on the couch while she went to the back to smoke her weed. About halfway into the movie, she came out and said she had to pick her kid up from daycare. She said, "I'll be right back. When I get back, I'll drop you off at home." I said, "Okay," and continued watching the movie.

About 5 minutes after she left, Carl began to rub on my leg. I sat up and said, "What are you doing?". He said, "What's wrong?" Then he put his hands around my neck and began to kiss me. For a minute, I engaged in kissing him back. After a few seconds I pulled away. All of a sudden, it seemed like the temperature in the house increased to 100 degrees. I was so nervous. He was a very popular person around the school, he played sports and had the girls. I didn't want to look like a lame but I was uncomfortable. I mean I knew Carl and he was cool but I didn't look at him as being physically attractive. I only looked at him as being cool, nothing more. The only times I've previously engaged in sexual activity was with my life long friend and my boyfriend. I've only known Carl for a few months but we weren't dating. This was extremely inappropriate. I said, "I think I'm just going to walk home.". He said, "Are you sure? She'll be back soon." I said, "Yeah, I'm going to go ahead and go." Then I stood up. He walked me to the door. He then grabbed my arm to pull me back and began to forcefully kiss me. He then pushed me onto the front door. I kept pushing him off of me, yelling stop! But the more I pushed and fought, the more aggressively he got. He looked me in the eyes and said "I like it a little rough, keep doing that!". He then picked me up and took me to the back room. He laid me on the bed and started pulling my clothes off. I kept fighting and pulling my pants back up. I was kicking, hitting and buckingling my pants back up as he kept unbuckling them. He somehow kept getting stronger. He managed to restrain both my wrists with one hand. He started kissing all over me before he slid inside of me. The harder I fought, the more turned on he became. He said "you might as well let me finish now, I'm already inside". So, I stopped and just let the tears roll down my face until he was done. I'm not entirely sure how long it went on. I just couldn't wait until it was over.

When he was finally finished, he let me up to get myself together. I felt so violated, disgusted, and dirty. I wanted to take my skin off. I ran to Osborn High to wait for my nieces to be released from school. I stayed on the side of the building, crying until I saw them walking past. When I spotted my niece, Keila, walking, I ran towards her in relief. She asked, "What's wrong? Why are you up here? Why are you shaking and crying?" I told her what had just happened. She instantly stopped walking and started crying with me. She said that I should tell the police and her mom about it. I disagreed with that idea. I said that I was skipping school. I'm going to get in even more trouble. I wasn't supposed to be over there in the first place. No one would ever believe me. I just want to go home, shower and go to bed. She went on to press the issue that I should tell her mom at least. I said no, I didn't want to. I was too embarrassed. I hated myself for putting myself in that situation. If I had never left school, that never would've happened. "It was all my fault," is what I kept telling myself. I couldn't go tell anybody in school. He was the man around school. He was very liked and respected by many. No one would ever believe me over him I thought. Nobody would like me anymore. I would just be putting my business out for everyone to judge me. I stopped hanging with the crew I was skipping classes with and started going to class more. The sight of seeing him made me sick to my stomach. Some days he even smiled at me as if we were still cool. He was antagonizing me at this point. He didn't speak to me but he always looked. I walked around with this secret for about a year.

A few weeks after this situation I started noticing discharge and a loud odor. No matter how many showers and baths I took, it was never enough to get rid of the smell. I started having extremely bad cramps in my abdomen and lower back. My urine was always a dark color and had a strong odor. I didn't think anything of this though. I just thought it was a part of becoming a woman. But the cramps started to become unbearable after some months. My menstruation time was the worst. I asked Terri if she could take me to the doctor to see if this was normal. I couldn't take it any more. She ended up taking me to a local Pediatrician doctor. After doing their assessment, they told me I had to go see a gynecologist doctor. Terri asked me if I was sexually active, I told her no. In my mind, I wasn't. I haven't had sex in months (since the day I was forced). The ped doctor prescribed me some Motrin to take for my cramps and pains. The cramps went away a little, but something still wasn't quite right. I didn't press the issue because the pain was slightly relieved. Some relief was better than none. A few more months went by, and the sharp pains came back. I hid it for as long as I could. By this time, the pain has been coming and going for about a year.

Now in the 11th grade, I was attending all of my classes (I never skipped another class since that traumatic experience). School, classes and grades were back important to me again. I barely passed my sophomore year. My gpa was only averaging at 1.8. I had received mostly D's and F's. I was lucky to have a C on my report card. In class, I even started sitting closer to the front instead of in the back. I was still cool with my old crew of friends but I started being more comfortable with being alone. I had more associates than friends.

Larry tried to talk to me before the summer break of the last semester but I wasn't feeling him at that time. The more I let him down easy, the more persistent he became. He was so sweet and always thoughtful. He always walked me to my classes, carried whatever I had in my hands, boufght me snacks, and always checked on me during class. He was the perfect gentleman. This is what I needed in my life. He ended up becoming my boyfriend fairly quickly. I was officially off the market and in a relationship. Life was coming around for the better this time around. We spent a lot of time together. I don't even think we had the same classes together, yet, somehow he was always in my classes with me, missing his own. Because he was an athlete and popular around the school, most teachers allowed him in when he wasn't supposed to be. We also had a lot of substitute teachers who didn't know who belonged where so he got away with a lot. People used to say we looked alike. I didn't see it but we got that saying often. He was so catering and warm to me. He made it easy to feel safe with him. I was looking for a male to love me after the passing of my father. He made it very easy. When we were ready to start having sex, it felt very uncomfortable physically. It hurt so bad; I could almost never let him finish. I thought it was because of the size of his penis or my inexperience was the reason for the pain. I just assumed it was supposed to feel like pain until I got used to having sex on a consistent basis. Although, the first two times I did it (consensual), it felt a lot different.

I had to go back to the doctor, but this time, I knew I had to tell the doctor the truth that I was sexually active. My boyfriend, Larry, and I decided to skip school and go to Herman Keffer, which was a free clinic hospital back in the day. If you ever see anyone here, it was never good. It was one of those places you had to disguise yourself in case anyone saw you inside. My STD results came back a couple of days later, stating that I had PID, which is also known as Pelvic Inflammatory Disease. The doctor explained to me that it was curable, but because I had chlamydia and gonorrhea for so long, it may have scarred or affected my cervix. He went on to explain that it may affect my chances of becoming pregnant or that I more than likely might experience miscarriages in the future. He said I was to take the medication as prescribed, and I should be fine. This news was devastating. I knew exactly where I got this STD because I only had sex twice before I was raped, and they both had worn condoms. My discharge, odor and cramps all started after I was raped. Which were all the symptoms of the diseases. This was a no brainer of who did this to me. I was so angry and hurt. This also saddened Larry. I told him what had happened with Carl. This was the second person I ever disclosed this information to. He told me that I should tell his parents because I didn't have a legal guardian. He told me I'd have to press charges and report this to the police. I didn't agree with this plan. I was even more ashamed of the situation. Not only was I violated, but I also had an STD that could possibly affect me bringing life into the world. "I may never be able to have a family,"

I thought. I was disgusted inside of my own skin. I wanted to jump out of my own body. How can a person do this to someone?

Larry was good at consoling me. He created a safe space to be able to talk to him just about anything. He loved everything about me. Whenever I was having one of my sad episodes, he would reassure me that I wasn't alone. Whenever I was moody, he allowed me to take my frustration out onto him. No matter what I was complaining about, he loved me even more. He even opened his family up to me. His parents were also heavily involved in my life. His sister became more like my sister. She was a year younger than I was but she hung around a lot of the upperclassmen. She was also an athlete. She ran track for the school, winning all types of medals and trophies. She was one of the best on our school's team.

Chapter 14

What's freedom?

Back at home with Terri, I wasn't as happy as I was before. The freedom to do whatever I wanted to do started to make me uncomfortable. We ate at fast food restaurants every day. My nieces and I started to argue a lot. I wanted more of my money out of the social security check. The $300 that Terri was giving me monthly wasn't enough for me anymore. My checks was almost $900. I asked her if I could receive more of it but she told me no because she had to pay bills with the rest. I asked her how was she paying the bills before I was there. We were all in a one bedroom apartment. I wasn't taking up that much space or running up bills to take $500. When she didn;t agree to give me more money, I reached out to the people I knew from my old neighborhood. I got in touch with Shalonda's cousin. Her family and I always remained close and kept in contact. I ended up moving in with Melissa and her 5 year old daughter. At the time, Melissa was only 24 years old. She agreed for me to live with her, giving her $400 of my money, and I kept the rest. The only catch was my bedroom was in her living room. I also had to babysit her daughter while she went to work. "This was a sweet deal," I thought. I didn't have to worry about sharing anything. There were no other teenagers around to argue with. I had the TV to myself because her daughter was always in her own room entertaining herself with her toys or watching her own TV. Melissa cooked often, so no more fast-food restaurants or receiving small portions of meals because there were 6 other people in the house. I still had to catch buses to school, but it was worth it. I was not changing my school, especially with me being in love with Larry at the time. Melissa lived near Finney High School on Detroit's east side, but I didn't care. I was not changing schools. I was back to getting good grades, and I only had a year left to graduate. I loved my friends, not to mention that Larry and I were closer than ever. I couldn't give all that up to start over.

While staying at Melissa's house, Larry and I grew closer everyday. We started seeing each other more outside of school. Somehow his dad convinced Melissa to allow me to stay some weekends. His parents even allowed me to sleep in his room, with the door shut, sleeping in his twin size bed. No one ever set us down to talk about sex or pregnancy prevention. They basically let us do what we wanted to do. They even let us drink alcohol with them. I usually always turn it down. However, one weekend I didn't. I ended up taking a few shots of 1800 tequila. I got intoxicated fairly quickly. As soon as I felt a buzz, I was ready to go upstairs to Larry's room. We went upstairs and had sex all night as if his parents weren't there at all. Nobody ever interrupted us. If they did, they would walk out and apologize. I always thought that this was weird but I was having fun with my boyfriend so of course I never questioned it. His dad would drive me all the way home to and from the east side so I wouldn't have to catch the bus. They lived down the street from our school. Our school wasn't deep west but it was still on the west side. It was about a 20 minute car ride one way. His dad would sometimes let us drive his car. He's the one who taught me how to drive in bad weather. He also made sure that we had date nights at least once a month. We went on mall dates, movie dates, restaurants and even a hotel. I can't remember how or why that happened but it did. Larry had two jobs, working at Subway and Burger King. If he wasn't working, or we weren't in school, we would be together..

Waking up one day, I felt extremely sick. I wasn't throwing up, but it kept feeling like I needed to. I couldn't eat or smell anything without feeling like I needed to throw up. Larry, being my best friend, I told him because he was wondering why I had decided not to come to school. He immediately said, "I'm about to skip school to come where you're at to take care of you." I told him he didn't have to do that; I'll be fine. He said, "I think you're pregnant, so I'm going to catch the bus to where you're at, then we're going to go to the doctor together." I laughed it off and said, "There's no way I could be pregnant; I think it was something I ate.". Besides, the doctor just said not too long ago that I would have reproductive issues, so there's no way I could get pregnant that quick. Larry caught the bus to my cousin's house anyway. That's where I was located at the time. When he arrived, we ended up walking to the nearby clinic. We explained to them what was going on, sharing my symptoms. After peeing in the cup, the doctor came back into the exam room and said, "Congratulations! You're pregnant!" Larry and I looked at each other, thinking, "What the fuck!" At this point in my life, too much was happening back-to-back. My head was spinning. The first thing he said was we had to tell his parents. I disagreed. I wanted to hide the whole thing, hoping it would just go away if we ignored the situation.

    I continued to live my life as if the doctor didn't tell me that news. I didn't tell anyone, no matter how sick I was. When Larry would bring it up, he would just make me angry, saying we had to tell an adult. I said I'll take care of it (knowing I never had an actual plan). Days, weeks, and now months went by, and I was still pregnant, and my stomach was getting bigger. The shit started to get real, so I had to tell somebody. I ended up telling Melissa. At first, she seemed disappointed, but she didn't seem like she really cared too much. She didn't give me any advice or talk to me about options. She only asked me, what was I going to do? I didn't know. I knew I didn't want to be a parent but at the same time I thought that it was a blessing. The thought of having someone to love me forever and I get to see them everyday brought me a piece of joy. I wasn't ready to be a parent but the doctor had just said not too long ago that I may not be able to have kids in my future and here I was pregnant. "was it meant to be?" I thought. The decision was completely mine. No one really influenced me one way or another.

I started staying at Larry's house more often because he said he wanted to take care of us. We were planning a whole future under his parents' nose and they didn't even know I was pregnant. I made him promise not to tell. I could tell that it was stressing him out, and how I was going about it was all wrong.I didn't feel right telling the world just yet. His dad stopped liking me because I started telling Larry he couldn't keep his dad all of his money from his jobs when we had a baby on the way. Larry always listened to me. His dad would take his whole check and only give him whatever he wanted to give him out of it. One time he stood up to his dad saying he didn't want to keep giving him his whole paycheck without an explanation. This caused a lot of conflict between the two of them. As a result of this, his dad started allowing two other neighborhood girls to come over behind my back. He wanted Larry to stop talking to me without demanding it. He did better. He started letting other girls come over to chill with Larry and his older brother. Basically influencing him to cheat on me.

Larry and I ended up breaking up because of this. I carried on as if I didn't have a whole life growing inside of me. I had no idea how I was going to take care of the baby on my own. By this time, I was at least 6 months pregnant and still trying to hide the pregnancy. I ended up buying my first car because I couldn't keep taking the bus to school while pregnant. It was too dangerous. Driving to school with my new car felt so damn good. I told myself, "I'm going to be a good mom. Look at me being responsible already." Rumors had gotten back to Larry's parents that I was pregnant. His dad decided to pay me a visit at school one day. As I was walking to my car after school, Larry's father pulled next to me and said, "So you call yourself pregnant, huh?". I was so disgusted with him that I ignored him and kept walking. He began to threaten and harass me the whole walk to my car. Once he saw me get in the car, he exploded, calling me so many names. He was being completely disrespectful. This caught me off guard because he never spoke to me like this before. I was so hurt by what this grown man was saying to me. No, I didn't have a plan to become a parent, but I knew I didn't want to kill my first child. He was going off on me so bad people were stepping in to defend me. He even jumped out of his car as if he was going to hit me. I couldn't wait to call Larry to tell him what his father had done to me. I didn't know whether to blame him for it or run to him for protection. After that incident, I kept my distance from Larry and his family altogether. I wouldn't answer any calls or texts from anyone associated with him. His father tried to apologize, but I refused to accept. In my mind, my baby and I were going to be alright with or without them.

About a week before my due date, Larry's parents talked me into moving in with them. We haven't seen or spoken to each other in quite some time, so it was easy to initially turn down their offer. But then I got to thinking, who would watch my baby girl while I go to school? Melissa worked the same hours I went to school. She can help me. The baby couldn't go straight to daycare. She would be too young. I ended up giving in and moved with them. They moved me right into Larry's room like we were a big family. I was going to the doctor frequently. The doctor started being extremely concerned about the health of the baby and myself. She said that my labor would have to be induced because she was getting too big for my body to handle. She said she was sitting on my lungs and that she was too big to move around. This visit made me so nervous. It was only supposed to be a routine checkup. I looked at Larry in distress. He looked at me and said, "Everything will be fine. I'm here for every step of the way." When we got back home, I asked him if we could tell his parents what the doctor said the next day. He said no at first, saying that this was a serious matter and I had to go that night. I told him how scared and unprepared I was and how my whole life was about to change. I asked if I could get one more day to mentally prepare for this. If my water broke or I started having labor pains, I would immediately let him know. He agreed to my request until the next day. The next day, he was ready to go tell everybody who had ears to listen that I was to be induced that day and meet our baby girl. We went to the hospital immediately after everyone in the house woke up.

Chapter 15
Ready or not

January 19, 2006, was the day I was in labor the entire day. I'm not exactly sure of the exact hours, but I know nothing was happening from the time we arrived at the hospital to about 11 pm that night. I guess my baby girl just wasn't ready to meet the world yet. Upon waiting, Larry's father was upset that I didn't want him in the labor room when the labor started. He said she was his granddaughter, and he had the right to be present. He made me feel extremely uncomfortable. Why would a grown man want to be in the labor room with his son's girlfriend while all of her body parts are exposed. I didn't have any adults present to take up for me and support me. I was a minor at the time. My doctor ended up standing up for me. She said she would not allow a grown man to be in a room with a child he had no rights over. However, I allowed Larry and his mom to stay in the room. After around 11:30 pm, I started having contractions. I was so high because they gave me an epidural injection in my spinal cord. During active labor, I asked Larry what time it was on his watch. He said it was about 11:58; why?" I was one push away from her being completely out of me. I said Okay, I'll wait a minute to catch my breath. When I saw it was midnight, I started to push again. On January 20, 2006 at 12:02am, Julia was born. I held her in on purpose so her zodiac sign would be an aquarius like my dad. I felt as if I would still be close to him somehow if my daughter shared the same zodiac sign as him. I also wanted her birthday to start at the beginning of the new day.

Right after I pushed her out, they allowed Larry's father back in the room. As soon as he came in, he whispered to the doctor. I heard the doctor say, "Excuse me? "What did you just say to me?" He looked at me then turned back to the doctor and said "Can we talk outside?" She said, "Sure." They both turned and walked out the door. About 2 minutes later, I heard the doctor and Larry's father arguing. Larry's mom opened the door, and I heard Larry's father saying, "We want a blood test on that baby today!" Larry stood up and said, "WHAT?" Larry went on to say, "What is going on?" The doctor came back to the room saying, "your father just asked me if I can do a paternity test on the baby. The baby is not even 10 minutes old." She said, "You were acting up about seeing this young lady's vagina about an hour ago, and now you want a blood test? What is going on?" Larry said, "I'm not getting a blood test. I knew she was pregnant before Julena knew. We have known about her being pregnant since she was 9 weeks pregnant. We just didn't tell you! I know this is my daughter for a fact. I even know the night I got her pregnant" The father said, "She's been gone for months. We don't know what she has been doing." Larry said, "I know what she has been doing. I'm not doing a test." They argued more then Larry's dad swung his fist at him. Larry ended up running from his dad. His dad began to chase him all through the hospital to fight him. Security was then called. What was supposed to have been a beautiful day turned into a nightmare quickly. I cried almost the entire day. When the Doctor first put the baby in my hands, I was scared. I had never held a newborn this tiny before. She was so small and fragile with a big head. She kept moving around, she was looking to be fed and she kept making sounds. Honestly, I was scared, so I instantly gave the baby back to the doctor and told her that I wasn't ready. Eventually, I had to get ready because visiting hours were coming to a close soon and I was going to be forced to hold her. Unless you were close kin to me, you couldn't stay with me after 8pm. For the entire day Larry and his mom did most of the work for me while I rested. They tried to send Larry home when visiting hours were over because he was technically an adult. He was 18 and I was 17 years old. After begging the doctor and nurses, explaining to them that I had no one but him to be there for me. I needed him to stay with me my entire time at the hospital. They emphasized and ended up allowing him to stay.

    I stayed in the hospital for a couple of days, but when I was discharged, I demanded to leave Larry's house. I'll just quit school if I have to do what I was thinking. I did not want to leave my baby in Larry's fathers hands. I didn't know what he was capable of, especially when I wouldn't be around. He apologized a few times about how he was behaving, but his voice made my stomach hurt. I strongly disliked him. I asked everyone I knew if I could stay with them until I found an apartment of my own. No one wanted a high school teenage mom and a newborn to live with them. I didn't want to go to a shelter, so I decided to return to Larry's house. I didn't stay long, though. I was extremely uncomfortable living under their roof. I think I stayed for about 2 weeks after the birth of Julia. I ended up moving back in with Melissa after begging her for so long. She was in a new house when I moved back in with her. She set up the basement for me to sleep in this time. She said she didn't want us in her living room like I was the last time I was with her. She said the basement was more suitable. At first, I didn't mind because I thought anywhere was better than being at Larry's house with his father. I stayed with Melissa for a few months but was uncomfortable sleeping in the basement with my newborn. It was too cold in the winter and there were too many spiders in the spring season. I started saving money to get my own apartment officially. Larry also started saving his money so we could do it together. By May 2006 we ended up moving into our first apartment on Detroit's west side off of Chicago Road.

    Here we are, two high school senior students with our first apartment and first car. 'It only gets better from here,' we thought. We continued to go to school every day. We even landed a job together at IHOP on Jefferson, which is towards Downtown Detroit. He worked as a busboy and I worked as a hostess. We both had help from our families babysitting Julia while we worked and went to school. He ended up changing schools so that gave us a little break away from each other. living together and working together meant we spent a lot of time together. We started to clash a lot. We needed to go to separate schools. Because of his credits and academic record, he had to attend an alternative school to graduate. We went to prom together and graduated around the same time though. Living independently wasn't as easy as we thought it would be, especially with a newborn. We stuck it out as long as possible, but it only lasted for about a year. Larry proposed to me, but it wasn't enough to keep us together, so we decided to go our separate ways and move out of our apartment. Neither of us couldn't afford the rent by ourselves. I moved in with my cousin back on the east side for a temporary time. When I left the apartment, I also quit working at IHOP.

While living with my cousin, I worked part-time at a local Popeyes chicken fast food restaurant, part-time at a plant producing plastic water bottles, and I also attended a trade school to become a medical assistant all at the same time. I was doing this for about a year until I graduated from Everest Institute with my Medical Assistant certificate. When I graduated, I did not find a job quickly like I expected to. I ended up quitting the plant job because it was too far and I was fired from popeyes due to the manager asking to take me out and I said no. He put $10 in my cashiers drawer and said I had too much money in my drawer and fired me the same day. He was in his 30's. I felt offended that he would even ask me something like that. I was happy to be fired. I continued to search for medical jobs but had no good luck. The Doctor's offices and hospitals were concerned about me being only 19 years old, with a toddler and fresh out of school. I searched for months until someone gave me the idea to work at a group home. A group home didn't need many qualifications to work. I just needed transportation. My first car transmission went out because I wasn't keeping up on the maintenance of it.

I didn't know anything about cars and no one told me I needed oil changes, coolant fluids etc. When I got my federal income taxes back that year, I ended up purchasing another vehicle. It wasn't the best but it got me to where I needed to go. Once I obtained reliable transportation, I was able to work full time for the first time. I worked as a Patient Tech Assistant in a group home for about 2 years. This was the beginning of my 10 year run in the medical field.

Throughout the next couple of years, Julia and I moved from different families' houses. Nobody really had room for us to live with them. We bounced around multiple houses and even were homeless for a short period of time. When we were sleeping in the car, I used to ask people if we could shower at their house or if I could get food to feed my daughter. Sometimes, I would ask if we could nap for a little while just to get my energy up to go to work. I became a workaholic. There was no such thing as too many hours to work. I was determined to get us out of that situation. Getting a sitter while I worked wasn't hard, surprisingly. Julia's grandmother Denise kept her alot. However, Larry was no longer in the picture at all. He would not help me with anything. Denise couldn't offer any financial support, but she was there for all the things money couldn't buy. Her husband and I still weren't on the best terms. I just didn't care for him at all. Eventually, I ended up getting my own apartment right in the same apartments my mom and I used to stay at when the apartment caught on fire when I was a kid. No one else would allow a 19-year-old to lease their own place with no cosigner. My cousin who used to live downstairs from my mom back in the day was still in contact with the owner of the building. She asked him if I could move into a unit to get me out of my homeless situation. To my surprise, he said yes. Unfortunately, it came with a cost. About 6 months of staying in my new apartment the landlord randomly asked if he could stop by to check on my plumbing. I invited him to come over on my day off. When he got there, he went on about how he remembered when I was younger and how beautiful I've grown up to be. He bragged about his involvement with the current Mayor of Detroit and that he had properties all over the city. He said he was one of the chief's of his police department and could pretty much do whatever he wanted in Detroit. He also reminded me that I was only 19 years old, and that no one would lease out to a person so young without a cosigner. He said I owe him a favor and he was interested in being more than a landlord or just a friend to me. This conversation took me by surprise and made me extremely uncomfortable. This married man had to have been in his 40s. His kids were my age. I asked him if he could please leave my apartment. He asked, "Are you sure you want to do that?" When I said, "Yes, please." I knew I had to find somewhere else to move to immediately.

Chapter 16
Adulthood isn't as fun as I thought it'll be

I ended up moving out of my apartment shortly after that uncomfortable visit from the slumlord. I moved back to the west side of Detroit but this time on W. Chicago and Greenfield. My brother and one of his close friends, Stephen, helped me move right away. After moving my things into my new apartment, Stephen asked me out on a date behind my brother's back. My brother made it clear for us not to engage or date one another. He knew that Stephen was the type of guy that I would typically date but Stephen was not ready to settle down at the time. He was just leaving a long term relationship with the mother of his first born and recently had a second child by someone else. Apparently he cheated on his current girlfriend with a side chick and got her pregnant. To my understanding, Stephen didn't want the second child because he was trying to make things work with his daughter's mom (the girlfriend). The side chick ended up giving birth to his son (his second child) anyway. His current girlfriend tried to accept his infidelity but wasn't able to stay in the relationship with him the more active he became in his son's life. The more active he became to his son, the further apart their relationship drifted. When I met him, he was living in his mom's basement. Although he was 5 years older than me living with his mom, I respected his situation. The relationship ending was so fresh and I knew it wouldn't take much for him to get back on his feet. I saw his potential to be a great man and possible husband to me. He seemed very mature, he had a nice job and he was very intelligent. His personality was laid back, he had great leadership qualities and he was family oriented. I was physically attracted to his dark skinned tone, his beautiful smile and the way he carried himself.

For some reason, I just couldn't resist Stephen's charm. I tried not to like him, but every time I saw him at my brother's gatherings, he made it difficult to do. We ended up dating behind my brother's back. Things advanced pretty quickly. My car engine went out in my car and I no longer had transportation to get back and forth to work within the first 2 months of us dating. He offered to move himself into my place so I could drive to work. We worked opposite shifts so this plan was perfect. My job was about 40 minutes away from my apartment and he lived about 30 minutes in the opposite direction. I wasn't going to be able to use his car with him living on the east side and I had to be at work everyday by 7am. I felt like I had no other choice, so I agreed. With us living together, he helped out a lot helping with all of the adult responsibilities I was just getting accustomed to. We tried to hide our secret from my brother and my family for as long as we could. Pooh ended up finding out after seeing Stephen's car parked at my apartment every day when he rode past my apartments. When he found out about us, he was extremely upset. But it wasn't anything he could do by then. We already started sharing our lives together full time. His two kids were coming over all the time. I was attending his family gatherings with him. We were having family days once a week with his 2 kids and my daughter. We were playing house and loving it.

A night before work, Ariel and I agreed for me to bring Julia to her house so I could go to work the next day. Ariel didn't like waking up early to get Julia. She said it was more convenient to let her stay overnight the day before my work days. Around this time, Ariel was babysitting Julia more (even though she is the only person who was making me pay to keep her) she lived the closest to me so I didn't mind. As I'm getting ready for bed, I received a frantic call from Ariel saying that Julia was suffering from a bad burn and that she needed to get to the hospital right away! She said it wasn't a good idea to wait for the ambulance and that I needed to get there as fast as I could and take her to the hospital myself. I got to her house within minutes of the call. Julia told me she reached for a pot on the top stove, trying to make herself some noodles. She said the whole pot of water spilled all over her arm. Another story was told by one of Ariel's daughters that she was in the kitchen cooking herself and didn't see Julia when she turned around. She said that when she turned around without noticing that Julia was standing right behind her, the pot of water fell on her. I'm not entirely sure what happened that night. I just know that the Doctors said that my daughter received second-degree burns on her forearm. Julia and I spent almost a week in the recovery of the burn trauma unit at the hospital. Larry said he wouldn't stay up there unless I left, and he and his new girlfriend could stay. Of course, there was no way this was happening, so once again, he wasn't there when we needed him most. Up to that point, he has not done anything for our daughter besides bought her a Dora the Explorer stuffed pillow, one pair of shoes, one outfit and he babysat her one time in her whole time of existence. Even after the accident, I still couldn't count on him to be more involved and active in her life.

This put me in a really bad place. Larry's dad and I weren't getting along because he blamed me for her getting burned. As a result, I didn't trust my daughter with her grandparents because he used to threaten that he would take custody of Julia from me. My other sister, Terri, and I were not on speaking terms because I was still mad at her for putting me out of her home just a year before. The same boyfriend that put my mom out was the same one that said a teenager and a baby cannot stay with them. They let me stay for about a week then told me that I had to go. This was the last home that I stayed in before I started sleeping inside of my car. Pooh worked the same hours as I did so he couldn't help out much. That left me with no babysitters. Although Steven and I were in a relationship and living together, I didn't want to dive into leaving my toddler with him so soon. I know that sounds crazy because we were living together already. Although Steven was pretty good with Julia and his own children when they were around, I wasn't completely comfortable just yet. After the burn, I became extra overprotective over her. But Steven was always active with our children. He took them to the park, often played with them, made their meals, got them dressed, and was overall a good father figure. I agreed when he offered to help me keep her while I went to work. To make me more comfortable, he often had his own children over to keep her company. We were really becoming one big blended family. Things were once again starting to feel like I could breathe a little.

Things were going good until I got pregnant. One day, we stopped by his parents' house for a regular visit, and his mom looked at me and randomly said, "You're pregnant!" We both looked at each other in a state of confusion, denying this allegation. I politely said, "No, I'm not." She said, "Good, do not get pregnant for him!" Right there in front of him. Little did I know, I was already pregnant. Up until that point, I had no signs of being pregnant. About a week after that visit, the signs came in full force. I started having really bad morning sickness and nausea. My appetite changed, I had mood swings and I was always restless. It was the weekend of July 4th holiday. I was with my family at a local park and decided to stop at the nearby dollar store to grab a pregnancy test. I took the test at the park. Of course, my results were positive. I called him immediately to tell him the news. His first reaction was, "What are you going to do?" with almost an agitated tone. This was a shocking reaction because I've always known Stephen to be a complete gentleman. He showed all signs of love, leadership and support. At the time, I had no idea what I was going to do. I just wanted to share the news. I was only 20 years old. I had no car, no sitter or help for the child I already had and I barely made it to work everyday. Besides, I just moved into my one bedroom apartment only a few months prior. I was in no shape to prepare for another responsibility.

For some reason, the only thing I kept thinking about was what the doctor said about how hard it would be to have kids. Here I was pregnant for the second time. I couldn't help but to think if this pregnancy was a blessing. My mom also told tell me to never have an abortion. She said it's one of the biggest sins besides suicide, and it could harm your body. I was scared as shit to make this life changing decision (again). I didn't know what to do. I thought, "What if I make the wrong one? How can I be sure I'm making the right decision for myself and my family?" So, I did what I always do when I needed answers. I prayed. I prayed very hard and was very careful with my words. Although I thought praying to God about abortion was completely out of line, I prayed about it anyway. I also started asking people their thoughts and their experiences about abortions and how they feel being a mom of more than one child. The logical advice most people gave was to get an abortion. It only made sense to get rid of an extra responsibility that I didn't need at that time. Some people said to keep the baby and they would help out more. I kept hearing in my mind, "All things happen for a reason. God makes no mistakes. How much faith do you have in the God you pray to?"

Steven and I talked and agreed to just have an abortion and be more careful next time. His behavior started to change. He started drinking more, talking to me in any kind of way, not giving me any attention, was irritable all the time and he started staying out late. When he didn't come home for 2 days without answering my calls or contacting me at all is where I drew the line. I knew it was the end of us. When he walked into our home, he said, "I was at my mom's house with my daughter, trying to clear my head." I knew this was a lie because I had already called his sister, who lived with their parents, earlier that day. She already confirmed that she hadn't seen or spoken to him in days either. I was actually more worried than anything else at first. But when he came through the door with the "clear my head" reason for going ghost, I couldn't deal with that. So, I gave him his belongings, opened the door to let him out and told him to call me when he had the money for the abortion. He was also supposed to take me to the clinic because I was too afraid to go alone and didn't have transportation.

Shortly after we broke up, I ended up losing my job. The doctor gave me medication to stop the morning sickness, but it left me drowsy and always feeling tired. I was caught sleeping on the couch on my lunch break at work and was fired immediately. Eventually, I fell behind on my bills and damn near lost everything I worked for including my car payments, rent, utility bills. I became depressed. Some days I didn't have enough motivation to do anything besides rollover in bed. I leaned onto God like I never have before. I was a pregnant 20 year old young lady with a 2-year-old child, with no help from anyone. I started going to church more. I started attending church multiple times a week. I was at the lowest point of my life (again) and I didn't know what to do about it. I was faced with being homeless again, but this time, my car was at risk of being taken from me because I had a car note that I couldn't afford to keep up with. Sleeping in the car again wasn't even an option this time around.

I didn't have anyone to call on for help. I couldn't go to Ariel's house after my daughter had been burned the way she was. Terri made it clear that I certainly couldn't come to her house being pregnant and having a toddler child. Pooh said I couldn't come to his home because his girlfriend he had at the time didn't like me. She didn't like how close my brother and I were. Almost every night I prayed and trusted that God had a plan. I randomly received a letter in the mail saying that I was approved for an apartment near downtown. It also said that my rental amount would be cheaper than my current rent at the time. They had a two-bedroom ready for move-in immediately. The apartment was nicer, the neighborhood was safer, and it was a step up from living in a one-bedroom apartment. I received my tax return earlier than expected that year. I was able to use my tax refund check to pay up to 6 months of my first rent upfront. My unemployment checks also started coming in. This blessing literally just fell into my hands. I knew it was all God behind this life changing shift. There was no other reason how this could have happened the way it did. I don't even remember applying to these apartments.

Chapter 17

Lemons and lemonade

When I moved into my new apartment, I had to figure out how I was going to catch back up on my car notes. I was so far behind, but I put all of my money into the apartment. I needed some security in case I couldn't find another job. I couldn't risk being behind on rental payments. I was already 6 months pregnant with no solid plan. Shortly after moving in, my car was repossessed. They gave no grace period to make up for late payments. The main thing that worried me about not having a car was how I was going to get to church and my doctor's visits. I told the pastor that my car was gone, so they arranged to have me transported for all of the services. Pooh and Terri both helped out by taking me to the doctor's appointments. All that was left for me to worry about was how I would raise two kids. With the due date approaching quickly, I didn't even have a bib prepared for the new bundle of joy. I had no money. Still, all I had was prayer and the word of God. At first, I tried looking for a job but didn't have anyone to keep my daughter. I didn't have guaranteed transportation to get back and forth even if anyone was to hire me. Not to mention that I was only several weeks away from my due date. Instead of continuing to look for a job, I took a CNA course instead. I figured having a Certified Nurse Assistant and Medical Assistant Certification together, I would have a better chance to get a job once the baby got here.

One day, Pooh came over to take me to one of my routine Doctor's appointments. I checked my mailbox before getting in his car, and there was a random $2,000 check with my name on it from a bank I was not a member of. This took me completely by surprise. How was this even possible? I thought it was fake, so I asked Pooh to take me to the bank just to confirm if it was actually real To my surprise, they cashed the check and gave me $2,000 cash. I immediately asked Pooh to help me look for a car. I said the baby would be here soon and we need a car! To this day, I still don't know where that money came from. I ended up purchasing a car with the money and was able to purchase a few things for the baby before his arrival. With all of these miracles happening before my eyes, there was no doubt in my mind that I made the right decision on not getting the abortion. God kept showing up in ways that I still can't explain to show me that I was covered and blessed.

I saw somewhere that walking increases the chances of having early labor. I was tired of being pregnant. I just turned 21 years old and wanted my body back. Julia and I walked a few miles for exercise just to increase my chances of going into early labor. We fell asleep and no more than a few hours later I was awakened out of my sleep with sharp contractions. A family from the church took us to the hospital. They were also keeping Julia while I was in labor. I trusted this family a lot. I viewed them as my own family. We've grown a great relationship over the period of time I was a member of the church. They were there for me in many ways. Stephen and I only had brief conversations throughout my pregnancy. I was extremely naïve thinking he would have a change of heart sooner or later. He wasn't with the other children's mothers but still stepped up to his responsibility is what I was thinking. There was no way he'd leave me high and dry once the baby got here. He loves kids. When we broke up, we didn't do anything too toxic to one another so he had no reason to never come around is what I kept telling myself. At the same time, I was scared to have another child and being stuck with raising two kids alone. I ended up reaching out to some people that I knew to explore adoption options.

Malik was born on April 26, 2009 at 5:11am. I had a 100% natural birth. After the back pain I was experiencing from giving birth to Julia with the epidural, I didn't want to do that again. I'd rather go natural than to make my back pain worse. When I first glanced at Malik, I noticed his left hand behind his head and his right foot hanging out of his little glass bed. I thought to myself "this is the coolest baby I've ever seen". I had to ask the doctor if everything was okay because he didn't cry at all. He barely made any noises. Which was a completely different experience than the first time. I fell in love. I had to ask myself, "What if Stephen never comes around? Are you ok with raising another kid alone?" The same doctor who delivered Julia was the same doctor who delivered Malik. As I sat there crying, she came in and spoke to me. She asked, "Are you ok?" I answered, "No," and just cried some more. She spoke life into me. She told me I couldn't believe in God, faith and fear all at the same time. She reminded me of the apartment miracle, the check miracle, the car miracle and the tax return miracle. She said, "Haven't God shown you he will make all ways for you. You just have to believe that God got you!". Her and I had grown closer over the years. She knew a lot of my personal business. Her telling me this brought confirmation that keeping my new bundle of joy was my only option. He was my blessing.

I got hired as a certified nurse assistant at a nursing home only 4 weeks after giving birth. I knew that my rent was getting ready to start back up. I had no time to waste on finding a job. It was time to hustle hard. Being at home for so long also made me more depressed. I don't think I gave my mind and body time to heal with the transition properly. All I kept telling myself was, "there's no way I could go homeless with two kids". When I started working, the church family would watch my kids. They had one daughter who was about 16 years old, and two sons (11) and (2) years old. They would keep my children no matter how long I was at work. I was back in my workaholic tunnel vision. I worked everytime they needed me to. All I was thinking was that I needed to catch up on 8 months worth of working. While working one day I randomly received a miracle call stating that my name was pulled for a low-income housing development. They said I was approved for a 3-bedroom townhome in Clinton Township and was able to move in right away. When I first applied, they said that the waiting list was up to 5 years long. I had only been on the waiting list for less than 6 months. Of course, I moved in right away.

Within two months of moving into our new townhouse, I purchased my first Truck with TVs in it. This was a huge step up from the life I had just a year ago. I purchased all new furniture furnishing my whole new home. God continued to show up in my life in ways I still can't give the full explanation on how certain things were possible. I wasn;t in the right places at the right time. I didn't do everything right. I didnt even pray for some of the miracles that I received. I didn't know how a way was going to be made, I just knew it was going to happen. There was no other explanation as to how all of this was happening to me within one year. I was finally about to care for my family financially. Still no help from either of the fathers. Stephen and I got into a physical altercation when Malik was a few weeks old.

We both attended the annual high school alumni. He graduated about 5 years before I did but the alumni was for all graduates of all years. When I spotted him, I was truly emotional and was going through postpartum. I acted out of rage, hurt and disappointment. He was with his second child's mother, drinking and having a good time. I walked up to him asking why he wasn't there for the birth of our son and what it was going to take to get some help from him. He shouted very loudly "that ugly ass baby isn't my baby! I make nice looking kids, you better find your baby daddy because I'm not him!". I slapped him before thinking about it. We started going back and forth arguing. My homegirl that I came with started fighting a girl that I didn't know behind where I was standing. By the time I realized what was going on behind me, his second baby mother (current girlfriend) was running towards me in attack mode. I beat her up and was attempting to drag her all through the school field. Stephen pulled me off of her and pushed me away from them. My homegirl grabbed me to tell me that the police were on the way so we had to go. When we got in the car I asked who she was fighting. She said it was his baby mother's sister. She was trying to sneak and hit me from behind when I was arguing with Stephen. She said she caught her and hit her before she was able to hit me to protect me. That's when they started fighting. I deeply apologized to her because that wasn't my intention. As I said, I was emotionally unstable. To this day, a lot of his family blame this incident for him not being an active father in our son's life.

Chapter 18
Finding another way

On a random day, getting off my 3-11pm shift, I asked my daughter, while bathing her, "Has anyone ever touched you inappropriately?" I'm not entirely sure what made me ask her that, but I did. To my surprise, she answered, "Yes." I had to ask her the same question in different ways until she finally told me the 11-year-old boy from the church family was touching her inappropriately. I instantly lit up. I felt like someone put a fireplace in the bathroom. All I saw was fire. I got her out of the tub and drove straight to the nearest hospital. There, we found out that her skin in her vagina wasn't broken. He did everything but penetrated her. From there, I drove to the police station to file a report. Unfortunately, the police said there wasn't much they could do because the accused was a minor. I contacted the church family to make them aware of the situation. Their reaction wasn't how I thought it would be. They didn't seem surprised at all, almost like no emotion. Their reactions were more of embarrassment, which told me there was more going on in that household. When I told the pastor, he also seemed as if he had no remorse. This experience left me "church burned". In other words, I wasn't feeling church anymore. I never lost my faith in God and Jesus Christ, but I thought I'd never go back to church again.

I was still working, but finding a sitter was extremely hard. I stopped working for the nursing home and picked up a group home job for better convenience. My daughter was old enough to attend preschool, but my son wasn't. There were times I had to sneak him to work with me. I'm not proud to say this, but it's true. There were times I had to leave him in the car while I went to work, going back and forth to check on him. There were days I hid him in the bathrooms, closets, or empty bedrooms if the patient had hearing or visual problems. I couldn't find a sitter while I worked but needed money to take care of my family. I felt like I had no choice. I couldn't depend on anyone. When I asked for help from my son's father or his parents, they always refused or simply didn't answer their phones. I felt my back was against a wall, and I had no choice. I was desperate and did desperate things. Looking at my son's face for the last time while hiding him in the car, he looked at me and cried with such a sad face. He knew he was about to get left in the car. He kept reaching for me to pick him up with a hopeful face and his sippy cup in his right hand. His eyes were saying, "Please don't leave me in here again,". This broke my heart. I quit that job that day and never looked back. I ended up finding another nursing home job when he was old enough to start preschool.

On April 10, 2011, I met someone. This someone was different from any other man I've ever met. He was charismatic, funny, romantic, charming and his skin tone was dark chocolate the way I liked it. As I was driving, I noticed someone trying to grab my attention at the stop light. At first, I ignored it, smiled, and kept driving. He was very persistent, so I gave in and shouted my number out. He called me immediately. We talked my whole ride to my destination and then some. We stayed on the phone talking for hours that day, the next day, and the days after. He made it very easy to fall in love with him. I wanted to feel wanted at 22 years old with a 1-year-old and a 4-year-old. Neither one of my kid's fathers was around. They never helped me, called to check on their child, and they both were completely absent. Organically, that put me in a very vulnerable and insecure state of mind. I felt unworthy, ugly, stupid, naïve and unloved. But when Rashawn came into my life, I felt accepted. He had a biological son of his own but accepted my children as his as well. I finally got the family I've been wanting.

After about 7 months into our relationship, things started to change. Rashawn stopped being kind to me. He began to cheat on me, disrespect me and abuse me. He was verbally, emotionally, mentally, and physically abusive. He was the kind of guy that tore me down to lift me back up with gifts, apologies and dates just to tear me back down. This started to become a routine of ours. Just to name a few things we've been through... He would completely humiliate me whenever he wanted to. He used to give his side women my address. He vandalized my car multiple times so I wouldn't be able to go to work or take my kids to school. The police caught him in the act while slicing my tires. They did nothing but told me to stop and go home. He hid inside my apartment and waited until I got home after leaving me downtown with no ride home. I didn't have my purse, a phone, any money, or no way to even get in touch with someone to get home. His sister found me and brought me home. Upon arrival, he was hiding in my son's room. Before I was able to understand what was happening, he was fighting me. There were a lot of times I covered bruises, scars, busted lips and bite marks. He threatened to kill me if I ever truly left him for good and said he would take my children. He said things like my family doesn't love me anyway so I wouldn't be missed. When he drank alcohol things were much worse. He would show up to my family members' houses if I was visiting them just to threaten and try to fight me. He went to my brother's house and told him to his face that he would kill me. All of this was going on and we never even lived together. He had his place for his other women and mine to sleep at when he felt like it. He even moved his child's mother into his home. He wasn't discrete with his cheating at all. He would lose his mind if he ever thought that I was even looking at anyone else besides him.

I dealt with this for about 4 and a half years. I finally had enough courage to move from my townhouse. I knew if I stayed there, I would never escape him. So, I secretly moved without him knowing (so I thought). I ended up quitting the nursing home and finally started working at a hospital as a medical assistant. I was finally doing what I loved and went to school for. I also enrolled into a community college to pursue an occupational therapist field. When I moved, he kept calling and begging for us to get back together. My oldest sister, Terri, had just passed away a few years ago. Going through the loss of her showed me how precious life is and how quickly it could end. When Terri passed away, that took a big chunk of energy out of me. The last time we had spoken to each other was when we had an actual physical altercation. I still blamed her for my mom's death. I carried that hurt with me for years. I blamed her for not being there when I needed her. I blamed her for not loving me the way I needed her to love me. But not in a million years would I think that would be my last time seeing or talking to her. One day, when I was at work, I got a call from my other sister, Ariel. Ariel and I don't speak much, so when I saw her name come across my caller id, I knew something wasn't right. When I answered the phone, all I heard was her crying. I instantly knew it was about Terri. I had a dream about Ariel dying a few nights before. In my dream, Ariel was lying on the side of her bedroom, naked, when someone found her. I didn't think much of it besides it being just a dream. I had intentions of calling to check on her but it slipped my mind. To hear Ariel tell me that's exactly how Terri died broke me down.

    I haven't had a death dream in years at this point. It was then I knew that my death dreams had come back. This was a hard reality to accept. I need more time. I needed to apologize to her. I needed to forgive her. I needed to hug her. I needed to see her to tell her how much I loved her. I was just so angry the last time I saw her because I saw her mimicking our mothers bad decisions. I was hurting but used my anger to show emotion. I didn't understand that she was deeply hurt too. All these years, she had been coping in her own way. She knew momma longer than I had, so she was probably hurting even more. I wasn't there for her the way she needed me to be, either. I was too busy fighting and being mad at everyone but not really understanding that everyone had their own lives. I felt like the soft womb that was starting to heal in my heart had just reopened. When my sister passed away, it opened a double grief. When I went to the morgue to view her body, I started asking questions about my dad's death. In my early adult years, I didn't have much mental space to properly heal and accept the people that I lost. I almost pretended like it never happened. That's how much I thought of it.

It was then that I discovered that for the past 8 years, it had all been a lie. I was told that my dad died in his sleep and my cousin was the person who supposedly found him. That story never made sense to me. I discovered that he never received an autopsy. It was documented that a request was made not to have one done. I also discovered he was not buried like my aunt told me. He was actually cremated. This would be the reason the whole family disappeared on the day of the funeral. I was never given the address of the burial site despite the million times I've asked her for it over the years. She always told me she'd have to find the cemetery information. It was like I just lost two people at once. When I asked my aunt about all of the information that I found out, she said that everyone was lying. She said that he was buried, and she didn't know what I was talking about. The funeral home told me it's documented that he had no children, and that's why she received the ashes. She also denied that and called the police on me to leave her property. After a few days, Ruth called me to tell me that she did have his ashes, but she spreaded them all over the Georgia River. This still didn't sit well with me. I felt this wasn't the truth either. I couldn't fight with her or prove it, so I just listened to her. After a few more days, she called me back and said she actually did have his ashes, but she would not give them to me until she died. She said she would put it in her will. I was devastated but also learned that I may still have a piece of my daddy somewhere on earth. That was satisfying enough for me.

When I bought my first home, I knew I owed it to myself to grow up and stop living in the past feeling sorry for myself. I had to forgive people who never apologized to me. I had to officially grieve and heal properly. I was determined more than anything to have a better life for all 3 of us. I ended up Leaving the hospital position and started working at an orthopedic surgeons office that was closer to my new house. I had a paid-for Cadillac sts rare colored pearl car. I had a new job that paid more than I ever was paid and I was the first black female my surgeons have ever hired. I was free from that past toxic relationship and ready to see what else life had in store. I started modeling, I got a night job as a waitress, I started prompting parties/events, I was a social media influencer and I became a ring girl for professional fights all at the same time. I was getting paid from all different directions. I started to become popular on Instagram and facebook so bookings were falling into my lap easily. The more popular I became, the better the opportunities were. Sometimes people would play with my money because I was handling all of my affairs on my own. I realized that I needed a manager to assist me with my bookings. I saw a guy named Rick managing certain models, so I reached out to him to see if he would also help me with my projects. He agreed, and we started working. He was my muscle man when certain promoters would try to play with my money. He made sure all of that was canceled. My popularity also grew quicker with him being behind my bookings. Our business relationship turned romantic over time. The more we worked together, the closer we became. He was damn near my best friend. He was persistent in pursuing me, and he became a huge part of my everyday life. I was single for about a little over a year since my last relationship, so I thought I was ready to love again. Although I didn't particularly find light-skinned men attractive, he was exceptional. He had brown hair, green eyes, and the cutest stomach. I fell in love with his personality; he was intelligent, selfless, caring, compassionate, and extremely thoughtful. He was also an entrepreneur. I've never dated a full time entrepreneur before. This was sexy to me.

Chapter 19
This is where it begins

Up to this point, I didn't know anything about being a full time entrepreneur. I was only doing gigs for a side hustle. Nothing to take seriously and make a life out of it. He got up everyday whenever he wanted to. He went to sleep when he wanted to. He made more money than me and my time was restricted. I know I'm not the brightest bulb in rooms, but this wasn't adding up to me. I worked 7am-3pm or sometimes 5pm Monday through Friday, to only bring home roughly $2,000 every other week. He sometimes made that in a day. Up until I got with Rick, I never thought of owning a business or being an entrepreneur. I assumed to be successful in life, you had to work in corporate America. To own a successful business is the white people league so somebody like me would never have a shot. I didn't know much about Rick's business besides the fact that he sold retail. I knew I didn't want to do anything like that, so I had to figure out what I could do.

Working multiple gigs all while having a full time job wasn't working for me anymore. I was away from my children too much. They weren't able to participate in any sports. I always had to leave them home alone. I had to figure out another way to make a living. I had already invested 10 years of my life in the medical field, and I wasn't far away from graduating as an occupational therapist assistant. However, for the first time in my life, I envisioned myself out of the medical field. The medical field has always been a passion of mine because I felt that I was too young to help my parents when they needed it. I'm now capable of helping someone else. Helping people has always been my absolute purpose. There is no doubt in my mind about this. "What's a better way to help people outside of being in the medical field?" I thought. I had to go back to my roots and pray about it. I wanted to make another life changing decision. I couldn't do it without direction. I started going back to church again. I actually started a few years back, around the time my sister passed away. But that church also left me a little scared. A lot of the services were about money. The church before that one mostly talked about how much God shames sinners. Churches were starting to look more and more phony to me. Nonetheless, praying was always there.

I ended up giving another church a try. I started going to this popular church called "Truth". From my first visit there, I felt at home. I felt like the puzzle fit perfectly. As Rick and I became more serious, things in my life aligned perfectly. Rick's mom suggested that I do a "fast" with the church. For those who aren't familiar with fasting; it's giving a sacrifice of things you love for the greater good and cleanse. Praying and getting closer to God is the purpose of doing a fast. You have to have a will to starve your weakness (distractions) with God's word and faith. I decided to do the fasting this year but I put my own twist to it. On my first fast, I sacrificed all red meat, alcohol, TV (if it wasn't biblical), radio (if it wasn't biblical), and social media. During this time, I prayed hard every time I thought about anything that I sacrificed. This took much discipline and obedience (something I wasn't used to having). I prayed on the way to work, from work, at work, at home, and pretty much anywhere at any time. I needed directions and protection. I wanted more in life but didn't know how to get it. The only way I knew how to get it was to go through God, so I did. I fasted and prayed for 40 days.

During those 40 days, I thought I could get into the beauty business for a change in career. At that time, doing hair was extremely profitable. I went to the nearest beauty supply store to grab everything to make wigs. I spent about $300 on supplies, a mannequin head and hair. I didn't even complete the whole wig before quitting. I knew that just wasn't my lane. I asked my cousin, who was already a licensed esthetician, how to do what she does. She said it took her 18 months to go to school. I thought that was too long. I didn't want to make that kind of commitment. I wanted something right away. So, back to the drawing board I went. Then I thought, "Maybe I can do nails." I ended up signing up for a basic nail class. When I went to the class, I knew right away that this wasn't my lane. I couldn't mix the acrylic with the powder and create a nail to save my life. I started becoming extremely frustrated and discouraged. I had no talents. I knew nothing outside of the medical field.

While in school one day, I got this bright idea to take a placement test. Something I should've done a long time ago. I'm not entirely sure why I didn't do this in the first place. Here, I am almost done with the requirements to graduate to second guess my decision. The test suggested that I should study business first, motivational speaking then nursing. In that order. You can only imagine how this left me even more frustrated. I decided to take it again just in case there was an error. The results came out exactly the same the second time. I was thinking of becoming an entrepreneur, but owning a business was something I had never thought about before. So, I asked God what does this mean? As I continued to go to my job every day. I became increasingly unhappy. There was a presidential election going on with Trump that had the whole nation divided into a racist war. I was working with all white people. Most of our patients were also white. They did not hold back how they felt about blacks and anyone else who wasn't white. They didn't care if I was around or not. They would express how much they did not like other races and how much they didn't want us in America. They would say things like Muslims should not be allowed to pray in public. Or black people don't deserve to have Medicaid. I started to hate going to work, and it showed in my performance. A lot of the time, I would go to the bathroom and just cry and pray because I didn't know what else to do. My job was too important to me for me to let it go.

I used to get my lashes done all the time. I used to get the individual lash clusters that took approximately 20 minutes to apply. Sometimes, I'll go on my lunch break at work or my cousin would do them. The last time I got them done, I developed a pink eye. I was way too old to be walking around with a pink eye. I spoke to my cousin Tasha about the pink eye situation, and she suggested that I get "lash extensions". At that time, I had no idea what those were. She said that they only cost around $85-$100. They are waterproof, they look natural and they last a lot longer than the regular individual lashes. I said, "Yeah, all of that sounds good, but who's paying $85 for some lashes?". She said, "Or don't get them and be bold.". That's all it took for me to try these extensions out. I had a birthday trip coming up to go to Vegas with Rick. This would be our first vacation together, I needed to look my best. Everything that Tasha said was true except the longer-lasting part. The lashes lasted for about a week. My family, friends, and I had a cake fight for my birthday, so I had to wash my face. As I washed all of the cake from my lashes out, the lashes slid right off with it. I was upset because I was told that they would last for weeks. I contacted the lash tech and told her what happened. She offered to give me a free set, but I hadn't decided not to go. I just thought, "Maybe next time, if I have an event coming up, I'll try them again. Besides, it took two hours to get them done. I didn't have that kind of time. That was really the end of me ever thinking of lash extensions again.

About 4 weeks after my birthday, I randomly had a dream. In my dream, I was a lash tech performing a lash set on a client. We were laughing and talking. It looked as if I was really enjoying lashing her. When I woke up, I told Rick about my dream. He brushed it off and sayid "go for it!" in a nonchalant tone. I spoke to Tasha about it, and she said that there was a class coming up with a local lash company. She thought I should give it a try. She said that the class was only $900. I laughed and said who got $900 just lying around for some lash class? There has got to be another way. She said you could YouTube it, but she highly suggested not doing that. After all, I just had a pinkeye myself not long ago from a lash service. "Would you trust yourself doing lashes on strangers without proper training?", she asked. This made sense to me, so I came up with the money and registered for the class. After failing at hair and nails, I was hoping this would be my big break.

I felt a sense of satisfaction from the moment I entered the classroom. I had no doubt that I was supposed to be in the class. I loved everything about it, from the art of the techniques, to the people I was in class with, to the teaching from the instructor. I was truly intrigued. I needed to learn more about this. There were so many different ways and styles of lashing that I wanted to learn more about. Immediately after class, I called my best friend at the time to ask if I could practice with her. I had already been in class for over 9 hours but my adrenaline was still high. She agreed that I could practice on her and met me at my house. When she got there, it took me about 3 movies to do her lashes. Our boyfriends actually watched 3 movies in the basement while I was doing her lashes behind them. I thought, "This is too hard. Maybe this isn't for me." But that thought quickly vanished away. I loved it too much to give up. I knew I just had to keep working at it. When I returned to work, I asked if I could shorten my days to focus more on home (my lashes). My supervisor told me no and said if I wanted more time off or wanted to go part-time to just quit. He said there was no room for part time employment.

After that meeting, I went to my desk and typed up a formal 2-week resignation letter. This surprised them because I had just gotten a raise, my benefits were great, and I had been there for years. Not to mention, I just got a brand-new car not less than a month before. I didn't care about any of that. I wanted to step out on faith and trust God. A wise person told me it's plain stupid to say that you trust God and be afraid in the same sentence. You can't have both. You have to either have faith or be afraid.

I saw a Steve Harvey video called "jump". That video changed my entire life. In this video, Steve Harvy said something along the lines of "every successful person in this world has jumped. You are eventually going to have to jump.. You cannot just exist in this life. You have to try to live. If you wake up every day believing it's more to your life than it is, then believe that it is. But to get to that life, you are going to have to jump." He said "when God created life, he gave us all a gift at birth. He never created a soul without endowing them with a gift. You have to quit looking at gifts as a sport or entertainment. It's more than that. You have to identify that gift. When you see people in life doing wonderful things, have you ever thought that maybe this person has identified their gift and is living in their gift? Because the bible says, your gift will make room for you. You can go get an education, that's nice. But if you don't use your gift, that education is only going to take you so far. So many people have degrees that they are not using. The secret is the gift. The only way for you to sorrow is if you have to jump! You have to take that gift that's on that backpack sitting on your back, get on that cleft, pull that cord, and jump.". He said "

That gift will open up and provide the thrive. If you don't ever use it, that gift will just sit there dormant. And if you just get up and go to a job every day that you hate going to, that is not living. You're just existing. At some point in your life, you should see what living is like. You have to keep in mind that when you first jump, your parachute will not open right away. You're going to hit some rocks, obtain scars, cuts, scrapes, and bruises. But the good news is that the parachute has to open.". he said "That is a promise from God. God's promises are true. If you think about it, you cannot name one thing that God has not gotten you through. And if he hasn't gotten you through it yet, he's currently bringing you through it now. So, if God has never left you hanging, why would he not allow your parachute to open? It has to open! You can play it safe and deal without the cuts and scars, stand on that cliff of life, and never jump. But here's another promise: your parachute will never open. You'll never know what God really has for you. God has a plan for you." He went on to say "God's promise to you is, I promise to give you life, and I promise to give your life more abundantly. If I were you, I'd jump because that's the only way to get to that abundant life. You have to take a chance. You can say to yourself, I have bills and responsibilities, but newsflash, whether you stay on the cliff or jump, the bills will always be there. At one point, go see what God has in store for you. God will hold you up, not let you fall. He didn't bring you this far to let you fall. Before you leave this world, do yourself a favor and jump one time.". Since watching that video, I've been jumping ever since. I have no regrets about any of the decisions that I've ever made.

Chapter 20

Jumping

After quitting my job, I started doing lashes full time. I started off working inside someone else's salon. I worked there for about 9-10 months before quitting to work in my basement. The larger my clientele grew, the more I wanted to do. I wanted my own shop, had my own supplies and started teaching my own classes. Rick believed in my vision. He surprised me with my own business suite for my birthday on April 3, 2017. This was one of the best things anyone could have ever done for me. I will forever appreciate him for believing and pushing me to be great. When I moved into my suite, blessings started falling in my lap. I invested thousands of dollars into finding the right products. I started teaching classes. I sold my own products and conducted my own business. Rick reminded me all the time of how the first few businesses always fall but I was blessed to have my first business thrive. I was passionate about my art and I loved what I did. Everyday was a good day at work for me. I was living a prayer that I prayed for. My dream was actually my reality (literally).

With all of this going on in my life, my aunt, Ruth, ended up passing away. Once again, I knew she died before I received the call. I haven't spoken to my paternal side of the family in years, so I'm not sure how my gift worked for this particular situation. As soon as I saw my cousin post on my Facebook page saying "call me, it's important", I knew instantly that Ruth had passed away. I would be falsely telling the story if I didn't tell you that one of my first thoughts wasn't my father's ashes. I was indeed sad about losing my aunt. I was very hurt by her transition. I also didn't want to sound insensitive about my request for my father's ashes, flag, pictures, and anything else that was my dad's right away so I waited for about a week after the funeral before requesting it. To my surprise, no one knew what I was talking about. Everyone swore they had no idea that my dad was cremated, and there were some ashes lying around. Everyone claimed that we all had the same story, that he was buried. They also said Ruth never had a will. I was furious. I didn't believe anyone. I had my suspicions, but it was then that I knew in my heart that Ruth was definitely hiding something and Spring was involved with it.

At Ruth's funeral, I felt the energy when I saw him. I had not seen that man in over a decade, but as soon as I saw him and looked him in the eyes, I knew wanted to tell me something about my dad's death. He had so much guilt in his eyes when he looked at me. He seemed to want to tell me something so deep to get the weight off of his shoulders. I believe he just knew it wasn't the right moment. Honestly, even if he told me the truth at that time, I don't think I would have been able to handle it, so I didn't pursue it. I asked my younger cousins if they could find the ashes for me. They insisted that they had no idea where they could be and Ruth was possibly lying about it. I knew she wasn't, though. Something inside of me kept saying that they were in her house somewhere. I kept telling them to look in the house really good. Almost 2 years went by, and his ashes were never found.

One day, on the way to work to service my first client of the day, my cousin, Lonna, called me around 9am to tell me she must see me right away! I told her that I had a full work day and was running late to my first client. I asked if she could wait until I was off work to talk. She said no and that she would come to my shop to meet me. I had no idea what this could be about. I knew no one died because I didn't have the feeling or a dream. She met me at my shop in exactly 20 minutes. We pulled up around the same time. When she walked in, she looked at me, paused, and pulled my dad's urn from the inside of her coat. I instantly burst into tears. She started to cry. Even the client started crying. Finally, after a decade, I have something from my father to remember him by outside of my own thoughts. I was overjoyed. From that day forward, Lonna and I became extremely close. We spoke from time to time before this day, but after this day, we spoke almost every week. We started becoming sisters/cousins again. In my mind, I owed her everything. If she ever needed or wanted anything that I had, without a question, I would quickly give it to her.

Rick proposed to me. We were on our way to the altar after over 3 years of being together on and off. Lonna was one of the first people I called to give the good news to. She was so supportive of our relationship even when he and I weren't. Of course, I asked her to be one of my bridesmaids. Rick and I had taken almost 11 months break from calling each other boyfriend and girlfriend. We were still romantically involved with each other during that period. We were still celebrating holidays and birthdays together. He was still spending nights over, and we even took vacations together. We just let the "title" go until we both figured out what we wanted to do. Rick wasn't a bad guy. He had his flaws like anyone else. Deep down, I knew we weren't meant to be together because we could never get along for a long period of time. We weren't equally yoked, and we saw life through two different lenses. During our first couple years of being together, we dealt with a lot of toxic situations; including arguing, infidelity, communication issues, lack of support, grief, partying, mental health, financial battles, immaturity, domestic altercations, intoxication situations, in and out of jail and so much more.

When he proposed and wanted our relationship back, he came back with a lot of corrections. He wasn't perfect, but he made the necessary adjustments to become a better man. He came back with a ring, goals and a promise. He lived up to his promises in many ways. His changed behavior didn't go unnoticed. I respected and fell in love with him more for taking on the leadership of redirecting our paths. But deep down, I was still hurting. I was still disappointed and angry with all of the stuff he put me through in the past but didn't know how to fully express it. I didn't know how to heal and process this new change. I didn't know how to forgive him without holding his past mistakes against him. It was almost like I had to tell myself everyday to forget the past ever happened but my pain wouldn't allow me to. It was a battle I was fighting with my mind and my heart. Entering back into this new relationship, I assumed time would heal. Here stands a new man in the same body ready to marry me and be mine forever. I didn't throw a lot of our past in his face, but I acted differently towards him. I wasn't happy and it started to become harder to hide after about a year into our engagement. I tried to be happy and fake it but you can only pretend to be something that you're not only for so long.

The things he changed were great, but it made other things more visible that maybe I was blinded to before. I started to notice our financial issues. We never lived together before we were engaged. We just always spent over nights with one another. When he moved in, we had agreements on how the bill payments would go. There were many times bills went into late payments. When I was paying the bills by myself I never was late so it brought me anxiety being behind. We both also had deep-rooted depressions that we never fully dealt with or healed from outside of our relationship. He turned to alcohol to deal with his pain. Before I met him I wasn't a fan of drinking alcohol. I dealt with my pain by keeping myself distracted, shutting the world out and pretending as if the memories or problems never existed. When we got together, I started dealing with unhealed pain through going out partying, traveling, drinking alcohol and social media. Other words "showing my ass". For years I wanted to be seen. I wanted to be heard. I wanted to be felt. I had so much built up inside of me and hidden from the world. When I started receiving a little attention, I became addicted to it. People started to see me but not for what I wanted them to see me for. They started to see my coverup. I still hid my scars and bruises because those were too embarrassing to show the world. I wanted to be seen as the girl that everybody wanted or wanted to be around. I started to lose myself to the idea of being popular. I knew I was hurting but didn't know how to heal. It was years of pain that I had tucked away and never spoke about. I thought if I didn't speak about it, it made it less real. Unconsciously, it was eating me up inside.

The drinking and partying became heavier over the years. We had two different visions for our lives. I wasn't comfortable with who I was becoming. I'm not great at lying but I had to become great at pretending. I was so unhappy with my life. I wanted more good to happen to and for me. I didn't want to pretend to be happy anymore. At the time, I had people in my life that kept putting mirrors to my face. Making me see myself for who I was. I didn't like the person who was looking back at me. My life wasn't where I wanted it to be and I had nobody but myself to blame for it. That was the hardest pill I think I've ever had to swallow. It's so much easier to blame other people for bad things that happen to you but to say "all of this is because of your own self" is a huge accountability nobody likes to face. It was time that I needed to grow up and stop settling for what I saw in front of me and go after the unseen possibilities I knew I was capable of getting. Of course I wanted to be married and to be settled down. I just wanted to make sure that the person I say "I do" to, I never regret it. I only desire to be married once. I feel like I waited so long to get married, I have no errors for choosing the wrong person. I should know exactly what I want from a person and I should be able to pour nothing but good into them. I wanted to be full of life so whatever I do for them, I would be overflowing with what they already have and vice versa. I didn't want us to empty each other's cups to give to the other person. That's exactly what Rick and I were doing. I would sacrifice my happiness for him and he was doing the same thing for me. We didn't realize that was the very thing that was hurting us more.

I wanted to move to another state, and he didn't. Most times, instead of fighting, we wouldn't speak to each other for days in the same house. Our house wasn't a home. We started to become roommates. Rick didn't really like my son either, which also put us in a bad space. Don't get me wrong, my son was a handful. He has caused me more hurt and disappointment than anyone else has in my life. But he was still a child, my child. Sometimes, I felt like I had to choose between the two, which wasn't fair to anybody. He loved my daughter, and my daughter loved him like he was her own biological father. She even went to school saying she had the same last name as him. She has Larry's last name but she never liked it. She begged me to change it all the time. I believe Rick was Julia's first love. They had a bond I thought was inseparable. He never missed a daddy's daughter dance, track meet, birthday, school event or anything. Julia was Rick's top priority. She absolutely adored him. Their relationship was priceless. Something that I've always wanted her to have. I had it with my father so I know how it makes a little girl feel to have that father figure who treats you like a princess. He always made sure that she felt special. She needed this because, again, neither of my children's fathers was around. That's another reason why I stayed as long as I did with Rick. Although he never had any biological children, he and his family accepted me and mine as their own.

With the love that Rick and I shared with one another and with our families loving each other as much as they did, I assumed that was enough to continue to rebuild our foundation. Our foundation continued to fall apart because it was standing on empty cups (brokenness). As I stated, instead of arguing, we just wouldn't speak to each other. Which is worse than arguing. Before we were engaged at least we argued when we communicated to see how the other person was feeling. Not speaking when something was bothering us made everything much worse. We only had sex maybe once a month (on a good month). Sometimes we slept in the same bed, sometimes we didn't. We stopped having date nights unless it was a special occasion.

We tried marriage counseling and church, but that didn't last long. We weren't putting our best efforts into saving the relationship. We were comfortable being in each other's lives and didn't want to start over with someone new. We had too much invested to throw it all away forever.

Although we were both entrepreneurs now, I looked at him as superior because he has always been in this business life. However, when it came to showing me the basic entry level as an entrepreneur, he didn't show me much. Most of the things I've learned were through trial and error on my own. I resented him for this not fully realizing that maybe some things he actually didn't know. When he started his businesses, he started with other people. Everybody had a role to contribute to their business so he probably didn't know how to do everything on the back end. I felt I wasn't a priority to him without fully realizing that he had his own thing going on too. He wasn't really successful in his field at the time and was trying to find his own way. But because we spoke less, there was only room for resentment to grow. I never sat and thought about what he was going through with his own business. I only complained about the financial shortage we had. I will admit that I played a major part in failing to communicate, especially towards the end of our relationship. I completely checked out of our relationship without even telling him. That wasn't fair to him, the kids, our families, and everything we built. I owe him an apology for not being mature enough to express what I was going through. I behaved very immaturely and selfishly. I never wanted to hurt anyone, including myself. It took a lot of self healing, growth and accountability to forgive myself for how we split.

Chapter 21
The importance of accountability

After leaving that relationship, I had to do some deep, spiritual healing and soul searching. I needed to be alone and figure out who I was, what drives me the most and what actually makes me happy. I have been in and out of relationships since a teenager. I could no longer look for happiness from other people. Seeking in others what I didn't have in myself no longer worked for me. Even seeking what motivated me to want to do better had to change. Since I became a mother, my kids have motivated me to go harder. Now that they're almost adults, I had to realize that I had to find other reasons to live. I decided to just choose me. I used to think that was selfish to say. Not anymore. I choose to find everything I look for in others, inside of myself. I stopped looking for validation and approvals from people. I take advice from others to use it for improving myself but not validation for acceptance. There's a fine line between the two. Loving me more is something I would never regret. I'm not just loving my pretty good side, I'm loving my ugly scars as well. I remind myself everyday that I am not my mistake. Everything that happened to me, also happened for me. If it didn't happen, I wouldn't be able to encourage you today. I spent most of my life finding someone to love me when I didn't truly love myself. The only way I could love myself was to spend time with myself, build a relationship, and find out who I am.

I made a lot of mistakes along my journey, but I embrace it now. I take that back. I didn't make mistakes; I had to learn lessons, and what better way to learn life lessons outside of experiences? Experience is the best teacher.

Over the past few years, I've learned how valuable peace of mind is. I am very intentional with what I feed my mind, my memory bank, my spirit, what I listen to, what I watch on television, the company I keep, the places I hang out at, the books that I read, the people I take advice from, the calls that I accept and what I entertain. My mental state of mind has been my number one priority. I have no desire to repeat anything that I once did. God must be in the front of every decision that I make. I'm not trying to force God on anyone, but I will say you have to believe in something. You cannot succeed in this world successfully alone. I have created thick barriers, covered unhealed wounds, didn't talk about past traumas, and cried alone because I have abandonment issues. I felt everyone was temporary, so why give people all of me? I had to realize that people are not just temporary; life is. If I continue living life, not giving it my all, I am robbing myself of a potentially good life. I'm old enough to trust my intuition. If something doesn't feel right, move accordingly. But if my intuition radar is not going off, why not use my opportunities to create potentially good relationships? I absolutely love who I'm becoming and how far I've come.

I have worked as a lash tech for almost 8 years to date. I grew my business from working in my basement to having my salon and people work for me over this period of time. I've taught over 400 students how to lash. I have my own lash product line. I've sold 1000's of lash products over the years. I've graduated as an aesthetician and received my esthetic license during the pandemic. I didn't do everything right forsure. I made some mistakes along the way. But my mistakes helped me grow as a person, a woman, and a business owner. I take pride in my company and what I've built. Lashjewels started as only a word written on a piece of paper. To a growing company that made over 6 figures annually. So many people told me that I was believing in a childlike dream for quitting the job that had the benefits and security that a woman of two children, with a home mortgage, a car note, and bills needed. I quit without a second thought the same day I was denied dropping my position from full-time to part-time. I prayed for it for this moment but I didn't prepare myself. I didn't have any money saved up somewhere. I didn't have a fallback plan or even another job lined up. I solely trusted God and God alone. I'm no more special than you. If you have read my whole book, you are officially a witness to the miracles God has brought me to and through. If it was done for me, it can and will be done for you. I had been "jumping" for years now. I'm no longer afraid of losing or taking a chance. Taking chances always either helped me grow and see where I needed to adjust or I got a win from it. Not taking chances always had me wondering "what if I did". Growth should always be the goal. Taking accountability for the bad as well as taking credit for the good opens up more blessings and opportunities to flow in.

My cousin, Lonna, died about a week before my birthday in 2022. I didn't foresee this coming at all. I knew she looked smaller, but I had no idea how much she was suffering. She had a rare genetic illness that she was battling with for years. I had no idea how severe it was until she was gone. During the pandemic, we grew closer than we ever have before. She would stop by my house and we would drink wine, watch movies, gossip, smoke marijuana, laugh and cry together. Out of nowhere about 3 weeks before her passing, I felt something come over me. I randomly texted her how much I loved her and admired her strength. I said I couldn't wait until our next girls' day and wanted to catch up on whatever she had been doing since I last saw her. She didn't respond immediately but ended up texting me the next day with a similar message. About a week later, I was told she was in the hospital, and she wasn't doing well. I was at work when I received the call. I had to stop what I was doing to call her directly. I FaceTime her, and there she was in the hospital. She laughed her way out of the seriousness of the conversation. She told me to have her favorite loaded potato meal ready for her when she got out of the hospital. We joked around for a little bit then I went back to work. About two days later, while I was looking for my son, who had run away from home, my cousin, Tasha, called me. For some reason, when I saw her number, I instantly knew it was about Lonna. I can't explain how or why I have these feelings; they just happen. Tasha informed me that Lonna died about 8 minutes prior to the call. My heart was shattered into pieces. She just celebrated her 27th birthday a few weeks ago. When I finally found my son, I rushed to the hospital. I was completely numbed driving there. It was that moment that I knew I was ready to leave Michigan for good.

In September 2022, I started renovating my home. I thought that if I changed the way it looked, I might feel better and want to stay. But I didn't, so I said to myself, "What if I move out and just buy a house on the west side. I'll be closer to my shop, and open up a second location?" That might satisfy my urge for wanting more. I wanted to move out of Michigan but my fear wouldn't allow me to think past "if I fail" thoughts. I didn't know anybody anywhere else outside of my hometown. After renovating my home, I started renting it out to Airbnb and VRBO. That didn't make me feel better either. I felt I was still missing something. I wanted something else. I wasn't satisfied. I was still hungry! In March of 2023, I told myself, "Ju, you have 12 days to get yourself together. That's all I'm giving you. Whatever work you think you need to do, get it done in 12 days." By this time, I had already retired from doing lashes. I still had my salon and other lash stylists working for me. After my trip from the Dominican Republic, I gave myself a deadline of March 31st to be moved out. I didn't know where I was going. I didn't have a job waiting on me anywhere. I barely had a car. I just turned my last car lease in and had no plans or idea of what I was going to do next. I ended up getting a new car lease the same day I had to turn my Alfa Romeo in. Again, this wasn't planned. I didn't want another lease. Over the past decade, I have driven Cadillac sts, 300s Chrysler, a Mercedes Benz crossover, and an Alfa Romeo. I had 7 days left before the deadline I set for myself arrived. I had to do something.

After getting another vehicle I prayed to God to bless my steps for what I was about to do next. I started packing my house up. I knew if I stayed comfortable, I wouldn't leave, so I rented a storage unit. I started moving most of our things there. Two days before my deadline, I called the realtor I hired to get his thoughts on how I should proceed with my house. I've had my house at this point for almost 9 years. I wasn't in a rush to sell it. He suggested that I do exactly that. He said to pack my furniture on a U-Haul and just go. I put some thought into it and went to sleep. The next day I woke up, I went to the U-Haul company and rented a truck. I packed everything I could fit inside the U-Haul and told the kids, "We are moving tomorrow!" Keep in mind that I had no destination or a job. The next day, I went to their high school and officially withdrew my son. I allowed my daughter to stay with her best friend for two weeks longer to finish her SATs. Once I left their school, I handled some more of my business before I got on the road. I hooked up my one-week-old vehicle to the back of the U-Haul and left. I drove for a total of 29 hours straight with only gas and food breaks. My daughter wasn't with me, so I drove the whole time by myself while my son enjoyed the ride. This particular U-Haul didn't have Bluetooth, so I had to get creative with the drive. I prayed a lot. I cried a lot. I talked a lot. After 29 hours of driving, I made it to Houston, Tx. When I got there, I started looking for apartments. By it being a late Friday afternoon, I was in a rush. I knew if I didn't find anything that day, we would be homeless at least until Monday. If you've read my previous chapters, you already know that being homeless was one of my biggest fears.

We drove around for about three hours, but we couldn't find any apartments that would accept us right away. Keep in mind, I had no idea how the Houston map or surrounding areas were set up. An associate of mine said, "Park the U-Haul at my house; I can take you to some places." She took me to some apartments near her house at around 4:30 pm. When I walked in the office, I fell in love. I desperately asked the manager if they had any 3 bedrooms available for immediate move-in. I told her my situation, but before I was able to tell her everything, she had already said yes. She said, "How soon are you able to move in?". I said "in about 15 minutes". She laughed and said they were about to close for the day. She said they could get me in the next morning as early as 9:00 am. After so many no's, I've finally gotten a yes! If that's not God's doing, I don't know what is. I was going back and forth about adding my last "jump" testimony in this book because I'm still living it. I haven't even been here a full calendar year yet, so this story is still being written.

What I can tell you is the Universe will always align with how you move rather it's good or bad.. My son started to have doubts about God and religion. I'm teaching my kids to have freedom of will. Now that he's getting older, I think he's starting to understand more. He doesn't have to listen to my stories and testimonials. He is seeing it for himself. I'm still unemployed. I moved to Houston with no residential address, and I'm paying all of my bills without missing or late payments. What other explanation could this be besides God's everlasting blessings? I believe that I'm being rewarded for the seeds that I planted. Every time I wake up, I tell myself, "I deserve this life. I'm grateful for this life. I may not have everything that I want, but I have more than enough". The secret is gratitude. The more you appreciate what you have, the more you'll receive. I had no idea where life was going to take me. I never lived outside of Michigan before. I just knew God wouldn't allow me to fail. Embrace all of the pain, the struggle, the story, the disappointments, the loss and the rain. Soon, the sunshine will come, it has to. The light at the end of the tunnel is closer than you think. You just can't give up or look back with regrets. Yesterday has already happened, tomorrow isn't promised to everyone, but today is here! I have not always been perfect, and I certainly have not done everything right, but I have never lost my faith in God, even on the days I had no strength to get out of bed.

We all have a story. We have all been through a lot. Whether you're rich or poor, there's a story to be told. My story may not be how you would write yours, but yours matters too! I decided to write a book to relate to teenage moms, rape victims, women involved in domestic violence, individuals who have dealt with grief and abandonment, suicidal thoughts, single parents, entrepreneurs, homeless individuals, and middle-aged people. I want you to read my story to know you're not alone. My goal is, if I can at least reach out to one person to make a difference, I want to try. My sole purpose in life will always be to help people and hold the door open for the next person behind me. We all need encouragement and inspiration. I hope reading my story will inspire you to "jump" out on a leap of faith. Even if it's one time just to see where life would take you. All you need is to have faith the size of a mustard seed. I'm not telling you something that I heard, I'm telling you something that I experienced.

   Reading my story, you couldn't help but to notice the little support I had. When no one was around to encourage, motivate, and help me, all I had was my prayer and faith. I'll be honest: I don't read my bible or go to church as much as I should. That didn't stop God from being covered, protected, and provided for from God. The moral of this whole story is God will make a way out of no way. Your greater is coming if you believe it. You will have everything you deserve if you understand the laws of attraction. Everything you think is married to how you feel. Even if something goes wrong in your day, it's okay to go through your emotions for a minute. But once your minute is up, it's time to switch your mindset. Life is too short not to take advantage of your moments. When the day passes, you don't have that opportunity again. You may see another January 1st, but not in the same year. Your best life is waiting for you. Go get it!

Printed in the USA
CPSIA information can be obtained
at www.ICGtesting.com
LVHW060016200424
777541LV00001B/9